The
TEACHING
LEARNING
ENTERPRISE

The
TEACHING
LEARNING
ENTERPRISE

Miami-Dade Community College's
Blueprint for Change

Mardee S. Jenrette
Vince Napoli

Foreword by K. Patricia Cross
Afterword by Robert H. McCabe

Anker Publishing Company, Inc.
Bolton, MA

THE TEACHING/LEARNING ENTERPRISE
Miami-Dade Community College's Blueprint for Change

ISBN 0–9627042–8–8

Composition by Deerfoot Studios.
Cover Design by Deerfoot Studios.

Anker Publishing Company, Inc.
176 Ballville Road
P.O. Box 249
Bolton, MA 01740–0249

About the Authors

Mardee S. Jenrette is Director of Teaching/Learning Advancement for the Miami-Dade Community College District and, since its inception in 1986, she had been Director of the college's Teaching/Learning Project. Prior to assuming these responsibilities, she spent fourteen years in the classroom as a professor of biology. Ms. Jenrette has made numerous conference presentations and consulted with many institutions on issues related to institutional support for teaching and learning. She has authored chapters in five books, published five articles on the topic, and serves on a number of advisory boards, including the National Advisory Board of the Fund for the Improvement of Post-Secondary Education.

Vince Napoli is Chair of the Sociology/Anthropology/Social Science Department at the Kendall Campus of Miami-Dade Community College, where he has been a faculty member for over twenty years. An original member of the Teaching/Learning Project's Steering Committee, Mr. Napoli chaired two of the key project committees and served as a consultant to several others. He is the co-author of two textbooks: *Systems of Society* and *Adjustment and Growth in a Changing World*.

CONTENTS

About the Authors   *v*

Foreword   *ix*

Preface   *xiii*

1. Context   1

2. Getting Started   15

3. Selecting the Issues   27

4. Organizing and Executing   39

5. Communicating   61

6. Institutionalizing Change   77

7. Helping People Change   101

8. Evaluating Outcomes   115

   Afterword   125

   Appendices   128

   Index   199

FOREWORD

This book is about far more than the Miami-Dade Teaching/Learning Project. It is about leadership, reform, community, and excellence. It is about a highly successful reform, carried off in an unlikely place, by (mostly) ordinary people. I use the term "ordinary people" here in the sense that Peters and Waterman used it in their best-selling book, *In Search of Excellence* (1982). In one of their more memorable quotes, they write, "For us, one of the main clues to corporate excellence is... unusual effort on the part of apparently ordinary employees." They add that "...associated with almost every excellent company was a strong leader (or two) who seemed to have a lot to do with making the company excellent in the first place...it appears that the real role of the chief executive is to manage the *values* of the organization" (emphasis in original).

In textbook-perfect pattern, the Teaching/Learning Project at Miami-Dade started with a statement of agreement about the values of the college, and went on from there to develop one of the most far-reaching and potentially powerful reforms of our times—times that leave us reeling from harsh and pointed criticism about the quality of teaching and learning.

On the face of it, Miami-Dade is not a likely place for innovation. Located in one of the most volatile urban areas in the nation, with a huge annual student population of some 120,000, a majority of whom report English as a second language, with five disparate campuses located miles apart in sections of the city that have their own distinctive characteristics, Miami-Dade would challenge the imagination and persistence of any aspiring reformer. Add to that the fact that Miami-Dade accepts for admission anyone who takes the trouble to register and offers them a choice of some 145 programs of study, hires up to 50 new full-time faculty members a year in specialties ranging from aircraft mechanics to philosophy, and I would conclude that implementing a project on excellence in teaching and learning is not what I would choose if I wished to enhance my reputation as a reform-minded administrator—maybe something more modest, like improving efficiency in the mailroom, or if I had lots of money to spend, achieving architectural distinction on the North Campus.

So these are not "ordinary people" who embarked on this remarkable journey across the land mines of reform. They faced not only the formidable task of changing the behaviors of individuals, but of then instituting a teaching evaluation process that passed the ultimate test of a referendum of the affected parties.

This is a book from the "working stiffs" who dealt with the day-to-day joys and frustrations of reform. Mardee Jenrette, before she became the full-time shepherd of the Teaching/Learning Project, was a biology teacher on the North Campus. While she enjoyed a reputation as a good and concerned teacher and a valued faculty colleague, she had no experience as an administrator and no burning "cause" as a reformer. Vince Napoli has been involved in faculty governance issues for more than 20 years at Miami-Dade, and he chaired some of the major policy and procedural committees in the Teaching/Learning Project. He teaches social studies on South Campus. In their résumés, they are "ordinary people." In their accomplishments, they are extraordinary. This is the story about the triumphs (and occasional failures) of the Teaching/Learning Project at Miami-Dade as they experienced it day-to-day. It is remarkable in its candor, sensitive in its insights, and objective in its analysis.

I had the unusual and wonderful experience of spending several months at Miami-Dade in the fall of 1987. I took a semester's leave from my post as professor of higher education at Harvard primarily because I thought it would be good for me to keep in touch with the realities that I was presumably teaching about. I chose Miami-Dade because I had long admired the presidential leadership style of Bob McCabe, I was impressed by the highly innovative work that Miami-Dade had done in using technology for thoroughly human aims, and I wanted to see for myself if this community college was as innovative and exciting as people said. I was also extremely interested, of course, in their new Teaching/Learning Project, but I did not know then that I would be witnessing a truly remarkable process in extensive and long-term reform.

My daily activities at Miami-Dade consisted of a few speeches and workshops, as well as the usual round of committee meetings and conversations with people pulled away momentarily from their duties to talk with the visiting dignitary from Harvard. What I did realize even then, however, was that there was an impressive staying power and commitment on the part of virtually all the task forces. They took their work very seriously; they were universally interested in learning whatever was known about their area of responsibility; they showed respect for one another; and most impressive of all to me, they showed incredible patience. They went back time and again to inform colleagues, solicit their opinions and advice, and incorporate their suggestions. I suppose I should have known by these signs that this was a reform that was going someplace, but it is only in retrospect that one can look back on the "big picture" of accomplishments. Most reform is hard slogging, dealing with little issues of big importance to someone, keeping track of endless details, and working step by step toward the larger vision that has an annoying way of disappearing in a fog of vagueness during committee meetings and planning sessions.

We owe a profound debt of gratitude to Bob McCabe for his vision and leadership, to Mardee Jenrette for her commitment and ability to keep the big picture in focus while dealing with the endless day-to-day detail required in a project of this magnitude, and to Mardee and Vince Napoli for distilling their experiences and accumulated wisdom in this volume. If we attend to what is said here, it is possible to learn from them without having to make every mistake ourselves. Most important of all, we can learn that major and far-reaching reform is possible for "ordinary people" who have the vision, commitment, and energy to make major changes in society.

K. Patricia Cross
Elizabeth and Edward Conner
    Professor of Higher Education
University of California, Berkeley

PREFACE

The Teaching/Learning Enterprise: Miami-Dade Community College's Blueprint for Change is written for all who are interested in improving teaching and learning in higher education. It is an action-oriented book. We offer it most particularly to college and university teachers, administrators, and support staff personnel who are in a position to initiate positive change within their respective institutions.

The book is grounded in reality, rather than theory. It provides answers to practical questions with respect to initiating, organizing, managing, institutionalizing, and evaluating educational reform. Most of the questions raised have been asked repeatedly for over six years by individuals who are interested in the Miami-Dade Teaching/Learning Project. In turn, most of the answers come from our direct experience with the project and not from books.

The first chapter differs from the rest in that it provides a brief but essential overview of the Miami-Dade project. Each of the other chapters is organized into three sections:

1. "Notes From The Miami-Dade Diary." This is a description of events related to the chapter's topic as they unfolded at Miami-Dade. This serves both as a focusing device for the chapter and as a background against which to place the material that follows in the next section.

2. "Critical Review." This is an evaluation of what we did and how we did it at Miami-Dade, including what worked, what did not work, and how and what we would change if we could start all over again.

3. "Discussion." This is a presentation of principles and practices related to the chapter's topic.

At the end of the book are three appendices. These contain materials such as memos, surveys, and agendas that were created by our hard working colleagues as part of the project. We have purposely emphasized "process" rather than "product" materials so that you may better understand the dynamics of the project. Appendix A is general in nature, presenting a variety of materials related to the project. Appendices B and C are more specific, containing materials that depict the evolutionary development of a particular area. Space limitations allow only a small portion of available materials to be included in the appendices. We hope that what we have chosen is useful.

This is not a book to thumb through at one sitting and then store on your bookshelf. Rather, it should be kept on your desk and used as a reference work. On the other hand, we do suggest that you read the book from cover to cover before concentrating heavily on any given chapter. By doing this, you will be in a better position to determine which starting point is appropriate for the specific set of circumstances at your institution.

This book is the product of the efforts of many people—too many to acknowledge in the space available here. However, we do wish to acknowledge the following individuals who provided us with excellent criticisms of the manuscript as we were developing it into a final form:

George A. Baker, North Carolina State University
K. Patricia Cross, University of California-Berkeley
Marilyn Fore, Horry-Georgetown Technical College
Patricia Hutchings, American Association for
      Higher Education
Betty L. Kyger, Columbia State Community College
Wilbert J. McKeachie, University of Michigan
James C. Palmer, Illinois State University
Michael H. Parsons, Hagerstown Junior College
Gordon Watts, North Arkansas Community College

We owe a special debt of gratitude to Flora Napoli, Suzanne Skidmore and Coral Jenrette for their patience, advice, and support throughout the project.

M.S.J.
V.N.

CONTEXT

The Miami-Dade Teaching/Learning Project is the manifestation of one college's commitment to examine its practices, to undertake fundamental reform, and to use all necessary resources in resolving issues of teaching and learning. The project was initiated in 1986 to address a set of problems that were about to have substantial impact on the institution. While the specific solutions outlined in the following chapters are, by necessity, designed to respond to the needs of Miami-Dade, other colleges and universities should find elements applicable and appropriate to their own settings. In addition, the processes Miami-Dade followed to resolve issues and build support for recommendations are transferable, along with many of the outcomes themselves. A description of the program should be of value to institutions with similar concerns.

This chapter provides an overview of the project, including its origins, goals, evolution, and significant products. It serves as a context for succeeding chapters that explore issues related to introducing and managing a teaching/learning project. Later chapters also expand upon material in this chapter and include critical commentary on Miami-Dade's project.

Conditions From Which the Project Arose

In 1986, immediately prior to the inception of the Teaching/Learning Project, the major issues confronting higher education were those that still exist today: an aging professoriate, an increasingly diverse student population, and changing emphases on effective teaching and learning. Robert McCabe, President of Miami-Dade Community College, was very much aware of the potential impact of these issues on the quality of teaching and learning at the college. First, like many institutions, Miami-Dade was projecting large numbers of faculty retirements in the 1990s. The college had many excellent faculty members, a significant percentage of whom had joined Miami-Dade in the 1960s and had spent virtually their entire careers in its classrooms. McCabe wondered how the college would find, attract, and retain high caliber personnel to continue the good work accomplished by retiring faculty. How would the institution's mission and values be communicated to these new faculty? Would it be possible to preserve the strengths, skills, and expertise of outgoing veterans? How could new faculty most quickly grasp and respond to the special needs of Miami-Dade students?

The second issue was the diversification of the student population. Higher education was being introduced to a new type of student—a student who would redefine the phrase "traditional student" for the 21st century. By 1986 the college's white Anglo majority population already had been supplanted by a wave of Cuban and other Latin American refugees. Its classrooms had been further enriched by a large African American population. More foreign students were selecting Miami-Dade than any other college or university in the United States, and over 50% of Miami-Dade students were reporting English as their second language. Would the learning environment thus need to be reexamined to ensure a quality education for these students at Miami-Dade?

A third factor of great importance to Miami-Dade was the growing volume of information on adult learning, learning styles, and cultural influences on learning preferences. Were there implications for the particular ways Miami-Dade instructors should teach so that Miami-Dade students could learn? How could the research on teaching be actively connected to teachers and their teaching? Another dimension was the increasing availability of affordable technology to enhance teaching. How could technology become an effective component of the Miami-Dade teaching/learning process?

In March of 1986, McCabe returned from an American Association of Higher Education National Conference in which he had heard K. Patricia Cross speak on her concept of classroom research. The presentation made a deep impression and crystallized for McCabe a method of integrating the issues of teacher retirement, nontraditional students, technology and research on teaching and learning. Cross had suggested that college-level teaching and learning would be enhanced if teachers were trained to conduct systematic classroom research on the effects of their teaching. By reflecting on the data, teachers could make appropriate adjustments in strategies and techniques so that student learning would improve. McCabe recognized that having teachers actively engaged in assessing their own work and the work of their students would be a way to begin a dialogue to improve teaching and learning. Once the dialogue began, many other doors would open. On the airplane home, McCabe began to formulate plans for what would become Miami-Dade's Teaching/Learning Project.

The Goals of the Miami-Dade Project

An effort with the planned magnitude of the Teaching/Learning Project is not one that can be entered into lightly, nor can the commitment be made in a single step. Therefore, the decision to embark evolved through a series of realizations.

1. Because of the complex nature of the issues, it was evident that "business as usual" was no longer a viable option. If the indicators were correct, and the 21st century was to be radically different, then making minor modifications to existing practices would be inadequate to meet the challenges facing higher education.

2. Support for teaching and learning was an institution-wide responsibility. What happened in Miami-Dade classrooms clearly would have to be a major focus of the planned project; however, the entire institution also would have to subject itself to scrutiny.

3. Those who did the work of teaching and learning, and thus possessed the most relevant knowledge and expertise, had a right to be involved in determining what changes would be made. They would also have a responsibility to become involved in the change process.

4. A basic part of the college's culture was a strong and pervasive institutional belief that Miami-Dade could achieve whatever goals it set.

Three goals were conceived for the project. They were interrelated and addressed the issues of fundamental importance to the college. The first and in many respects the overarching goal was to improve teaching and learning at Miami-Dade. Achieving this broad goal would require the college to focus on the increasing numbers and needs of nontraditional students. It would also help Miami-Dade to do that which every educational institution must endeavor to do—provide students with a high quality education.

A second goal was to make teaching at the college a professionally rewarding career. Achieving this goal would help to address the issue of replacing retirees with high caliber personnel who, like their predecessors, would choose to remain at Miami-Dade for significant portions of their teaching careers. To achieve this, it was clear that high performance standards would have to be in place to challenge faculty and to enable them to take pride in their accomplishments. Valued performance and achievement would have to be recognized and rewarded, and these rewards would have to be substantial and meaningful to faculty.

The third goal was to make teaching and learning the focal point of Miami-Dade's activities and decision-making processes. When allocating scarce resources, for instance, college personnel would be obligated to consider the question, "What impact will this decision have on teaching and learning?" This goal ensured that the project's arena for action would extend beyond the classroom. It also would send the message that establishing and maintaining a sound environment where teaching and learning could flourish was the responsibility of each member of Miami-Dade's faculty and staff.

Progress and Products of the Teaching/Learning Project

The project began with a series of activities designed to allow members of the institution to "catch-up" with McCabe's ideas on teaching and learning; to understand his rationale for the need to make changes; to measure their own ideas against his; and to extend his concept and add flesh to his skeletal proposal. This "catch-up" period extended for several months during the spring and fall of 1986, during which time McCabe solicited reactions to the proposed project and used those reactions to enhance and modify his original concept.

In late fall, a day-long "conversation on teaching and learning" proved to be pivotal in establishing the scope of the project and assuring participation of institutional personnel (see Appendix A16). Participants included thirty administrative and faculty leaders and five invited guests from outside the college. The day began with a single question posed to the group: "What should we do to improve teaching and learning at this institution?" As might be expected, initial responses to this question focused heavily on faculty, students, and their interactions in the classroom.

The thought that teachers alone would be affected by the proposed Teaching/Learning Project was quickly dispelled after an observation by one of the campus presidents. He related several recent encounters with faculty in which they decried the physical conditions of their classrooms: burned out light bulbs that went unreplaced; broken chairs that sat for months in the corners of rooms; no chalk for the boards. "I wonder what message that sends to teachers and their students about the importance of teaching and learning to this college?" they challenged him. That painful illustration opened the discussion to examine the vital role that administrators and all support services play in creating an environment conducive to effective teaching and learning. It was becoming clear that the project would be more complex, more comprehensive, more time-and-energy-consuming, and more expensive than McCabe had originally anticipated. It was also even clearer how critically important it would be to undertake the project.

By the end of 1986, a full-time project director and a twenty-two member, college-wide steering committee of faculty and administrators had been appointed. McCabe pledged that time would be given to do the job well, and he set aside a liberal budget for development. The Teaching/Learning Project was officially underway.

An early challenge for the Steering Committee was to determine how to manage the direction and activities of such a monumental endeavor, one that could legitimately address all aspects of the institution. At their first series of meetings in 1987, the Steering Committee agreed on four conceptual areas: institutional values, faculty excellence, the teaching/learning environment, and new faculty. They further determined that the work would be carried out by subcommittees of the Steering Committee, each created as needed and commissioned to focus on a single issue. Subcommittee membership would consist of faculty and administrators, and would be opened to persons beyond the Steering Committee members to broaden the opportunity for direct involvement of other institutional personnel.

The first area to be addressed was that of institutional values related to teaching and learning. This was particularly important because a clear delineation of the college's values would serve as a basic foundation for the whole project to build upon. Since their work was so significant, the Teaching/Learning Values Subcommittee immediately set about their task. They began with an intensive research review of college-produced documents, self-studies, and material written about Miami-Dade. From this review they identified implicit values which were then placed into a survey and sent to all college personnel as well as a sampling of students and community members. Several cycles of activity followed, including data refinement, obtaining additional input, and providing additional feedback.

By December 1987, a set of seven institutional values related to teaching/learning had been articulated. Accompanying each value were statements that illustrated how the college would make that value operational (see Appendix A11). This values document then became the cornerstone of the entire project. It provided not only a sense of direction but also a sense of boundaries, an essential context within which ideas and actions would be debated by all working subcommittees.

The second conceptual area, faculty excellence, also became part of the project's foundation. In order to foster and reward excellence, a common understanding of the term would be required. This would be accomplished by identifying the qualities and characteristic behaviors in Miami-Dade faculty that constituted excellence in service to students. Criteria could then be derived to assess prospective faculty, to review the ongoing performance of faculty, and to make decisions about tenure and promotion.

The Faculty Excellence Subcommittee began with current research on principles of learning and from that research extrapolated a set of indicators of good teaching. Turning their findings into a survey format, the subcommittee used a process of continually incorporating feedback from colleagues and responses to mailed surveys to revise and refine their work. The resultant twenty-nine item *Statement of Faculty Excellence*, first published in 1988, reflects contributions from faculty, administrators, and students and meshes with the institutional values (see Appendix B). It defines excellence as it applies to Miami-Dade faculty. The *Statement of Faculty Excellence* was so successful that processes to develop similar statements of excellence for support staff personnel, administrators, and department chairpersons were initiated. When all have been completed and adopted by the District Board of Trustees, Miami-Dade will have vivid and distinct conceptions of the qualities it values in employees throughout the organization as defined by the employees themselves. Further, those qualities will all flow from a focus on teaching and learning, providing a unifying perspective for the separate constituencies of the college.

The third conceptual area chosen was the teaching/learning environment. While highly skilled teachers and willing learners are required for excellent teaching and learning, high quality support services are also essential to create an environment which facilitates teaching and encourages learning. The physical plant must be properly maintained; appropriate supplies, together with equipment that is in good working condition, must be readily available; audio-visual, clerical, and custodial services must be efficiently rendered. In short, the commitment to excellence must be shared by all personnel whose efforts support the teaching/learning process, even in the most indirect way.

The Teaching/Learning Environment Subcommittee, upon conclusion of their research, recommended processes to ensure that support of the teaching/learning relationship would become part of the operational practices of all service areas. They suggested that user feedback be solicited; that faculty regularly be invited to talk with service providers; that annual objectives be established and include recognition of each area's importance to the college's teaching/learning mission; and, that items relating to those objectives be included in the annual performance reviews of all service area personnel.

Although the subcommittee completed their work in 1988, implementation of recommendations was neither immediate nor uniform in service areas across the college. Areas directly servicing the classroom found it easiest to scrutinize their practices vis-a-vis teaching and learning. The bookstores, libraries, and audiovisual services fell into this category. In contrast, the purchasing department, budget office, and personnel office, while just as vital, were further removed and therefore had to clearly understand their relationship to the teaching/learning process before they could respond.

The remaining one of the four initial conceptual areas focused on new faculty. Principles and practices for recruiting, hiring, and acculturating new faculty were reviewed, and many fruitful discussions emerged as the New Faculty Subcommittee tackled their charge. Groups were convened to discuss and identify the needs of new faculty, as well as the needs of the institution relative to new hires. Recent hires and twenty-year veterans shared their diverse perspectives as they responded to questions such as, "What did Miami-Dade do that was especially helpful as you began your career here?" and "What would have been helpful that was not done?"

The subcommittee recommended that the new values document and the *Statement of Faculty Excellence* be used as recruitment tools. Taken together, they would inform prospective applicants about the atmosphere at Miami-Dade and what would be expected of them as employees. After all, just as an institution carefully selects a candidate, so should a candidate carefully choose an institution. These documents would provide ample data to help applicants decide whether or not to go forward. It was further recommended that screening committees use the documents to design an interview protocol to elicit information about those critical aspects of the faculty role that a transcript cannot provide. In other words, a strategy was designed to focus on the central questions of whether a candidate knew the subject *and* would be able to effectively teach it to Miami-Dade students.

Once on board, there are many facets to becoming an effective Miami-Dade faculty member. One of the more important products in this area has been the creation of a pre-service New Faculty Orientation program. New faculty report one week before veteran faculty in the fall, and are introduced to both district and campus operations through workshops, presentations, and meetings conducted by appropriate personnel. New hires are given a separate contract, including pay, to cover this pre-service period. Follow-up orientation activities continue throughout the faculty member's first year on campus.

A second phase of orientation consists of a mentoring program. The program is designed to improve and accelerate the process by which new faculty become knowledgeable about the college, effective in their positions, and comfortable as members of the faculty. Each new hire is paired with a veteran faculty member; mentor and protégé then meet regularly for a year, refining the scope of their relationship as needs emerge.

As developmental work with the four initial areas was completed, second-tier issues emerged. Once teaching/learning values and the *Statement of Faculty Excellence* were adopted as official college documents, logic dictated that a review be conducted of existing personnel policies related to faculty. College policies and procedures should encourage the development of faculty and should reward those whose performance reflects excellence as defined by the values and *Statement of Faculty Excellence*. The comprehensive set of policies and procedures that was eventually adopted became known as Faculty Advancement. This document encompasses the annual performance review and the awarding of tenure, promotions, and endowed chairs to faculty members. The system governed by these policies and procedures rests upon three philosophical principles:

1. The system should be supportive and developmental in nature. Continuous monitoring of performance provides ongoing opportunity for reinforcement of positive efforts. It also encourages prescriptive intervention long before negative personnel action would normally be taken in cases where performance is below acceptable standards.

2. Important personnel decisions should be based on information obtained systematically and from multiple sources. Supervisors, students, and faculty members are in the position to make valuable commentary on faculty advancement decisions. Commentary from peers and other sources often will be relevant as well.

3. Individual faculty members should be responsible for their own advancement. Whether seeking tenure, promotion, or an endowed chair, the individual should provide evidence of professional growth, development and accomplishments. The teaching/learning values and the *Statement of Faculty Excellence* provide all individuals in the decision-making process with a common standard from which criteria can be drawn.

As these principles emerged, it became evident that the college would require a greatly expanded staff and program development function. Centers for Teaching and Learning were established on the four large campuses, each with a full-time director, support staff personnel, and a substantial budget. The Support for Faculty Subcommittee was created to review the work of previous subcommittees and to make recommendations regarding the role and program focus of the new Centers for Teaching and Learning. Along with more traditional activities (such as funding travel to professional conferences and providing workshops and mini-grants to faculty to help update subject area knowledge and to enhance teaching skills), the subcommittee recommended implementation of the following: 1) a technical component to the centers with hardware, software, and instructional personnel to help faculty use technology to improve their teaching; 2) program elements for all personnel, including staff and administrators as well as faculty, to reinforce the belief that teaching and learning are everyone's responsibility; and 3) a common, college-wide core of work-shops and consultations to assist personnel in accessing the Faculty Advancement procedures.

Two graduate-level courses were developed by Teaching/Learning Project subcommittees in collaboration with faculty from the University of Miami (see Appendix C). "Assessing Learning in the Community College" teaches skills in the collection and effective use of data obtained through classroom feedback and research techniques. "Effective Teaching and Learning in the Community College" explores, among other topics, the impact of learning style and cultural background on student academic performance and the teaching of critical thinking skills. It also helps faculty broaden their repertoires of teaching strategies. Under the tenure policy of Faculty Advancement, both courses are required of all new, full-time faculty as a condition of continuing employment. They are also made available to all other faculty as elective, developmental learning experiences. Since individuals take these courses while they are teaching, they have ongoing laboratories for experimentation, as well as help and encouragement from supportive peers who are their fellow students. The college pays the cost of tuition, and the University of Miami accepts course credits as part of a doctoral program. It is the responsibility of the Centers for Teaching and Learning to enroll faculty and to schedule sections of the courses. In addition, the centers facilitate continuation of the dialogue between new and veteran faculty. Lead faculty hold periodic "brown bag" get-togethers, informal meetings in which faculty can share their efforts to enhance student learning. Some centers publish newsletters and sponsor sessions which promote sharing of selected strategies with a larger faculty audience.

Other integral components of the new Faculty Advancement policies and procedures include the documentation of professional growth and development, and the attainment of standards for tenure and promotion through a performance portfolio. It is the responsibility of the Center for Teaching and Learning to train faculty in portfolio construction, assist individuals as they prepare their portfolios, and train tenure and promotions committees in the evaluation of portfolios against established standards and published criteria.

The Endowed Chair Program is considered by many to be the capstone of the Faculty Advancement effort. As the Teaching/Learning Project began, President McCabe instructed the Miami-Dade Community College Foundation to begin a campaign to raise an endowment large enough to support 100 chairs. Unlike chairs in a traditional university setting, this honor would be awarded to full-time faculty whose service to Miami-Dade students was outstanding. Criteria for awarding endowed chairs were derived from the *Statement of Faculty Excellence*. Faculty who wish to be considered candidates for a chair must present a performance portfolio to the Endowed Chair Committee for evaluation. Help in preparing an endowed chair portfolio is available to faculty through each campus's Center for Teaching and Learning.

An additional component of Faculty Advancement is a college-wide student feedback program. At the three-quarters point of each major semester, students are invited to give feedback to their teachers via an instrument based on those qualities from the *Statement of Faculty Excellence* that students can judge. Faculty use feedback data in their portfolios as one source of evidence that they have met required criteria. Chairpersons discuss feedback with faculty as part of the annual performance review. Faculty may consult with the director of their Center for Teaching and Learning as they discover, through the feedback process, skill areas that they wish to develop.

Because Faculty Advancement is such a radical departure from business as usual, the new system needed to be monitored and periodically reviewed for effectiveness. The Faculty Advancement Committee recommended the creation of a Monitoring and Review Committee. This group would be a standing committee composed of both faculty members and administrators. Their charge would be to ensure consistent and equitable application of Faculty Advancement policies and procedures by overseeing their application and reporting findings annually to appropriate bodies within the college's governance structure. The committee would also review the effectiveness of Faculty

Advancement procedures and every three years would make recommendations for changes to those procedures (see Appendix A6). Hence, a built-in self-correcting mechanism for Faculty Advancement procedures will tend to institutionalize change and extend the positive effects of the project indefinitely.

Faculty Advancement, as a concept, is such a viable and potentially powerful tool to improve teaching/learning and to recognize professional activities of faculty, that it is being adapted for all college personnel. A *Statement of Administrator Excellence* and a *Statement of Support Staff Excellence* have been developed. Each focuses on the roles of these groups in support of teaching and learning. A performance review program, including feedback from faculty, has been piloted for chairpersons and administrators, and a reward system built on excellence is on the drawing board for administrators and support staff. The Support Staff Advancement Subcommittee and the Administrator Advancement Subcommittee have adopted the same philosophical principles that guide faculty advancement: there should be a supportive, developmental system; important personnel decisions should be based on information obtained systematically from multiple sources; and individuals should be responsible for their own advancement.

As the work on Faculty Advancement unfolded, the special needs of nonclassroom faculty (counselors and librarians) and adjunct faculty became clear. The extra responsibilities thrust on department chairpersons, and the pressure on them to become faculty coaches and developers rather than evaluators, caused concern and prompted the commission of the Department Chairperson Compensation/Support Committee. Couple these new subcommittees with those already in operation, and it is clear why President McCabe began to refer to the Teaching/Learning Project as "The Project that Ate Miami-Dade" (see Appendix A19).

What began as an idea to focus on classroom teaching and learning eventually evolved into a project that would affect all college personnel, including full-time and adjunct classroom faculty, nonclassroom faculty, staff and administrators, as well as students. The project also affects all college operations, including budgeting, and it extends to plant maintenance and construction. The Miami-Dade Teaching/Learning Project represents a completely new way of doing business and, as such, is certainly the most far-reaching and important set of reforms ever undertaken by the college.

GETTING STARTED

A major institutional reform is most vulnerable at its start. There are not enough champions to face doubters, nor enough evidence to prove that what is envisioned will be accomplished. Who will start the project, how and when it will start, and how people will be encouraged to become active participants must be thoughtfully considered to ensure enough momentum to get the project safely underway.

Notes from the Miami-Dade Diary

June 1986

College President Robert McCabe becomes increasingly concerned about the number of veteran Miami-Dade faculty who will be retiring in the next decade, the increasing number of nontraditional students enrolling at the college, and the accumulating research on effective teaching that is not finding its way into college classrooms. The president formalizes these concerns by addressing them in a concept paper, *Organizing Miami-Dade Community College to Emphasize Faculty/Student Performance* (see Appendix A1).

In the paper, the president points out that several years of work have resulted in coordinated processes to advise, monitor, and direct students through their academic programs. Attention must be turned to faculty development in order to strengthen the teaching and learning relationship. The president notes, "...a system must be developed which is designed to expect good performance and to reward excellent performance."

McCabe goes on to state that it is imperative to develop and implement a program to recruit faculty with the best potential Miami-Dade "fit," to integrate research into the college's reward system (a reference to K. Patricia Cross' classroom research concept), and to relate achievement of college-valued outcomes to evaluation, tenure, and promotion. He outlines a series of goals to set direction for the fledgling project he envisions. Significantly, McCabe emphasizes that he expects, "the program will be developed and the ideas and concepts will be refined, adjusted, and shaped through an extensive and broadly participatory process. This is essential in order to incorporate the best thinking of the faculty and professional staff and to ensure the wide base of support necessary for success." He goes on to acknowledge that the project will require considerable time and care in development and implementation.

As he continues to outline a program, the president indicates he will establish a budget and appoint a full-time director who will report to him. He details areas he expects to see developed: agreement on teaching/learning outcomes; delineation of faculty behaviors which contribute to student success; a research base for evaluation and promotion; salary adjustments to support more stringent criteria; new faculty selection procedures; and a performance-based evaluation system.

Later in June 1986

McCabe invites 120 administrators and faculty leaders to a luncheon at an off-campus setting. He presents his ideas on teaching and learning and distributes copies of the concept paper. He challenges the members of the audience to review his arguments and to provide feedback on the proposed project within the next month.

July 1986

McCabe receives a positive response from the academic leaders of the college and initiates a search for a project director.

The applicant pool is limited to current institutional personnel. To make the pool as deep as possible, a job description is distributed via interoffice mail to all campuses and via U.S. mail to the homes of all faculty and administrators.

The job description reiterates the basic goal, "to ensure that teaching/learning is our central focus," and adds, "Dr. McCabe expects personally to give this project the highest priority, and the project director will report to him." Listed as necessary qualifications and interests for the applicant are demonstrated teaching excellence, facility with utilizing research data, knowledge of teaching and learning theory, writing ability, organizational skills, and knowledge of Miami-Dade Community College and commitment to its philosophy (see Appendix A12).

September through December 1986

The president delivers his message to a continually expanding group of supporters. In September, "Elevating the Profession" is published in Volume 39(1) of the *AAHE Bulletin*. In an interview format, McCabe discusses his concern about the failure of higher education to encourage faculty to concentrate their efforts on teaching. He shares his desire to relate faculty rewards and recognition to valued performance, and to provide supportive professional development programs for faculty so they can enhance their teaching skills.

In October, McCabe makes a presentation of similar content at the annual conference of the League for Innovation in the Community College. Within Miami-Dade, he addresses 100 faculty senators at the combined Faculty Senates' Fall Workshop, and reaches other faculty and administrators through sessions he holds on each of the four college campuses. General themes come into focus: 1) the need to improve teaching and learning; 2) the obligation of the institution to recognize and reward those who perform in an excellent manner; and 3) the desire to make teaching a rewarding profession for those faculty who are truly dedicated to the mission of Miami-Dade Community College. In each Miami-Dade meeting, faculty applaud his comments on raising the priority of teaching and learning and on restructuring the faculty reward system.

October 1986

Following a search conducted by a college-wide screening committee, a project director is named. The campuses begin to make nominations for a college-wide project steering committee. The process to build commitment continues with a day long meeting of thirty college administrators and faculty, some of whom will become members of the steering committee. The newly named project director participates along with five guests from other institutions of higher education.

At this meeting a wide-ranging discussion about teaching and learning adds shape and substance to the McCabe concept and produces recommendations on the structure and responsibilities of the project steering committee (see Appendix A3). It is after this meeting that the project gets its official name, the Miami-Dade Community College Teaching/Learning Project.

May 1987

McCabe holds an off-campus breakfast meeting for campus presidents, deans, and associate deans. The purpose is to share information about major thrusts at the college. The project director is the only speaker invited to share the podium with the president. The status of the Teaching/Learning Project is clearly communicated.

Critical Review

After almost a decade, it is possible to look back to the beginning of the project and identify decisions that enhanced successes and actions that created hurdles that would have to be overcome. The project's strong start can be attributed to numerous factors:

1. The president shared his vision, his hopes, and his expectations with college leadership.

2. The president coupled oral presentations with a written concept paper, minimizing the chance for misinterpretation of his ideas.

3. The concept paper outlining the project was clear in its goals and in the need for such an undertaking. However, it was intentionally left open-ended as to how goals would be

reached. Ample room was provided for others to make contributions.

4. The president communicated the collaborative nature of the project in several ways: he solicited feedback on feasibility; he held campus-by-campus meetings with invitations to participate; he used a day-long discussion to elicit specific recommendations; and he appointed a collegewide steering committee of faculty and administrators.

5. It was clear that McCabe was committed to and would wholly support the effort. He provided a budget, appointed a project director, and acknowledged that a project of this magnitude would take time. He underscored the importance of the project: The project director would be full-time and would report directly to him.

6. The president made his own commitment clear: He spent many hours of his own time sharing his thoughts on the project, and pledged to raise funds for salary increases if faculty pledged to examine their efforts and make changes as necessary to improve teaching and learning at the college.

McCabe's thrust for change was strong, but he left room for participation by others. Generally, he did an outstanding job working with faculty by providing the right amount of initial direction, commitment, and support, and then by taking a step back so that the faculty could assume their rightful responsibilities in the workings of the effort.

As mentioned earlier, the beginning of the project was a strong one, but improvement was possible. Consider the following:

1. A problem with the inclusion of administrators occurred at the mid to upper-management level. In the early stages of the project (and at other key points which will be addressed in chapters that follow), McCabe had effectively developed a strategy of going directly to the faculty to discuss matters of concern. He articulated his own position and spoke for the administration. This practice had the positive effect of communicating accurately to faculty the importance of the project and the importance of their involvement. Despite

these efforts, there was insufficient development of knowledge and commitment at the middle administrative levels
during the initial phases of the project. The lack of mid-level
administrator involvement had its most dramatic impact in
1991, during the first year of implementing faculty advancement policies and procedures. Facing a difficult transition
to a new system, faculty looked to their own administrators
for guidance. Many administrators were not in a position to
provide the support and reassurance that faculty sought
and needed. The implementation process was thus more
difficult and the responsibility for success was thrust on far
fewer shoulders than it should have been. (More about this
in Chapters 6 and 7.)

2. "Teaching/learning is everyone's responsibility," was a
   theme often repeated, yet support staff and non-teaching
   faculty were initially excluded from direct participation in
   the project. Several years passed before the role of either
   was clear in the overall teaching/learning effort. Although
   the mistake was eventually rectified, the transition was not
   a smooth one.

3. The only component of the proposed project that McCabe
   developed in detail was the establishment of Faculty Teaching Chairs. He specified the amount of the annual award,
   that the chairs would be awarded to outstanding Miami-
   Dade faculty, and that 100 would be sought. Several years
   later, as the faculty advancement component of the program
   was being developed, faculty wanted to revisit the detail
   and even the concept of an endowed chair program. The
   sense of faculty ownership in this component was weakest.

Discussion

An institution where all members are equally prepared to
embark on a project that will result in major organizational
change is rare indeed. But most institutions do have individuals
who are willing to: 1) change their own patterns of behavior
and challenge their own favorite assumptions; 2) put in the necessary time to make things work; and 3) take the risks that come
along with stepping into the unknown. One's personal decision

to get involved is essential, although it must be supported by institutional commitment.

There is no set of characteristics by which to judge how ready individuals are to take on an extensive project. Whether faculty, staff, or administrators; whether new to the institution or veterans; whether low or high on the organizational chart; individuals will support or perhaps oppose the proposed change.

Among the tasks of managing a successful project are: 1) gauging how receptive people are and then encouraging those already committed; 2) educating the unaware; 3) reaching and moving the knowledgeable but uncommitted; and 4) finding ways to protect the project from being disabled by those who disagree with the plan or who feel threatened by change. Knowing what to do, how to do it, and when to act are critical to a successful effort.

Determining Who Starts the Project

In our experience, whether the project's initiator is at or near the organization's top, or is a member of its grassroots, the objective is to involve people at all organizational levels. Without that involvement, the project will fail. A basic tenet is that everyone in an institution is responsible for the effectiveness of institutional teaching/learning efforts. However, individuals whose responsibilities lie farthest from direct delivery of instruction or direct support services to students, have the hardest time relating their day-to-day activities to the outcomes of teaching and learning. Often, it is with these constituencies that commitment has to be built as the project progresses.

Who starts, then? Probably those who are closest to the interface of teaching with learning (i.e., faculty) or those who are held most directly accountable for the institution's teaching/learning outcomes (i.e., upper-level academic administrators or the CEO). Individuals at these levels are typically more motivated to initiate the process. While either scenario is possible, the level where the effort is initiated will determine what will happen next. If the administrative leadership provides the impetus, faculty should be brought into the project early (see Appendices A13, A18). Wise administrators should furnish little detail and limit themselves to what they hope will be accomplished. Answers to the question of how to achieve stated objectives should be left for those who will be required to implement outcomes. This type of beginning is more ceremonial than substantive. The message to be communicated is that ownership must be shared; the venture must be a joint one. Bringing faculty in too late may seriously damage any prospect for a collaborative effort.

If faculty initiate the process, they must consider strategies that will effectively bring administrative leadership into the project. Without the commitment of administration, resources will not be available to bring about significant institutional change. Once again, ownership must be shared, but the timing of the administration's entry must be carefully considered. Faculty should first take time to develop an initial concept that clearly addresses relevant teaching/learning needs. Administrators, accustomed to taking charge, may inadvertently appropriate a project if they join it too early or too forcefully. If faculty involvement becomes tentative, the prospects for a collaborative effort can be seriously damaged. On the other hand, an invitation to join must be issued before faculty have committed to a concept that the administration is unwilling to support.

Knowing when to act is crucial. A sound sense of timing is important throughout the life of the project. This is especially true in its infancy, when the project has not yet developed to a point where it can be carried through difficult periods by its own momentum.

Determining How to Start the Project

Who starts the project affects how it starts. Also, the context within which a particular institution operates, its institutional culture, external factors, the depth and breadth of initial commitments, and a host of other variables all impact initial decisions.

Here are some of the more common ways of starting a project.

1. A senior academic officer or CEO circulates a concept paper within the institution. The paper outlines in general terms a set of problems and a goal; it then proposes an initial starting point to reach the goal. The CEO, through the concept paper, articulates a personal intention to act and defines what that action will be and when it will occur.

2. A senior academic officer or CEO delivers the same message orally at a meeting that is called specifically to introduce the new project. The message includes time lines for initial action as well as personal pledges so that the audience understands that subsequent action will occur.

3. Individuals are appointed and given titles that identify them as having responsibility for championing the new undertaking. This strategy will be associated principally with administrative initiative. It should *not* be a first step. Prior to any appointment of staff, the initiating individual(s) should present a preliminary proposal on which they should solicit and review feedback to ensure that there is sufficient support to proceed.

4. A group of faculty who have come together around a common need or interest area identify themselves. They may publish a position paper, speak at an appropriate meeting, or merely schedule an appointment with a CEO. The project begins when this group decides to go public and/or invite others to join in their efforts.

Determining Which Facets of Teaching/Learning Should Start the Project

Each decision has an impact on determining which strategies will be most successful in advancing the project to its next level. For instance, knowing who will start a project affects how the project will start. Where it will start (i.e. which teaching/learning issues will be addressed first) influences these earlier decisions as well. Answers, of course, are specific to each institution, so outlining a series of additional areas on which to reflect may assist you in building an effective institutional plan.

1. Do not be misled by the tendency to begin the project by tackling your institution's greatest teaching/learning needs or problem areas. First consider if basic conditions have been satisfied that will allow you to address these needs head-on. Is the cost of what you want to do more than you are willing to bear at this time? Are the people who need to be involved ready to participate?

2. Consider beginning with an activity that has the greatest likelihood of success. Such a starting point offers an outcome you want and the success you need to provide momentum.

3. Ask yourself what actions will be seen as potentially yielding the greatest direct benefit to key players in the institution. If administrators initiate the process, starting with development of support and/or recognition systems for teaching excellence is a strategy that will help encourage hesitant faculty to extend themselves. For faculty initiated proceedings, starting with a strategy designed to directly enhance student learning will get the attention of reluctant administrators.

4. Decide how much of a commitment you are willing to make now. This question must be asked and answered at every institutional level and by every individual who participates in your endeavor. Limits must be clearly set and just as clearly communicated. Too many good plans fail and are assumed to be poor when the real problem is one of timing; i.e., too much ambition built on a resource-poor base.

Determining When to Start a Project

A project can start when the following conditions have been met: there are enough people committed to achieve initial objectives; those individuals are available to participate; and it has been determined that the non-personnel resources needed are available.

As attractive as it may seem to begin, if the necessary ingredients are not present, there is more to be lost than gained by a premature start. In the long term it will be easier to delay a start than to recover from an initial failure. However, it is also possible to be too cautious; change implies taking risks. Your project should be initiated when there is a reasonable chance of success.

When Key Personnel Are Not Ready

When individuals are not ready, they may initially respond by not volunteering to participate. If pursued, they may persist in withholding support. If you argue, they may counter with reasons why they cannot participate or perhaps they will suggest that the idea proposed is a poor one.

An upper-level administrator can require participation which will quickly add numbers to the project. However, what is needed is honest involvement, not mere compliance and certainly not passive resistance. Waiting for key players who are not ready to begin is one strategy, but not the only one. It is legitimate to encourage involvement by helping to create a genuine desire, concern, and interest among individuals.

Here are a few suggestions on how to be encouraging.

1. Introduce a concept, then wait. Give listeners (or readers) a chance to mull over new ideas, to formulate and ask questions, and to become comfortable with the concept before you ask them to do anything. Administrators should be prepared for a "let's wait and see if this is real" attitude from faculty. Only time can prove that the commitment to a major undertaking is a serious one. If the goal is behavioral or attitudinal change, you must be patient; change takes time. A personal commitment to the project must be demonstrated continuously if you expect others to commit themselves. (More about this in a later chapter.)

2. Make sure yours is the voice people hear. Do not trust your words to be passed on by those who do not yet share your vision and enthusiasm.

3. If you are faculty and the involvement of upper-level administrators is being courted, go slowly. You might start by asking an administrator to say a few words at an appropriate meeting. Settle for lip service commitment at first; it should be easy to secure. (Who could say that he or she is *against* teaching and learning?) If you are concerned about the message being accurately communicated, it might be better to ask if you can have some agenda time. Always remember to present the concept yourself if the vision is not yet shared.

Just as faculty can be challenged to accept change, so can administrators. The strategies to reach the two groups may differ, but the outcome can be the same—more people honestly committed to an institution-wide teaching/learning effort.

3

SELECTING THE ISSUES

The complexity of the teaching/learning relationship suggests the need for a careful analysis of issues. Questions concerning relevance and importance, as well as a number of others, must be asked as part of any process to identify the teaching/learning issues that will be addressed by your project. Involvement of key institutional personnel is also key to a successful outcome.

Notes from the Miami-Dade Diary

October 1986

The first substantive teaching/learning meeting is held. Members of the new Project Steering Committee participate along with campus academic deans, presidents, and faculty senate members. Invited external guests are Nancy Armes (Dallas Community College District), George Baker and John Roueche (University of Texas, Austin), K. Patricia Cross (Harvard), and Terry O'Banion (League for Innovation in the Community College). The commitment to a full day on the topic, the presence of college leadership and respected guests, and President McCabe create an air of excitement and a sense of the importance of the meeting.

The thirty participants are divided into three task groups and are given an overview of the concepts of the Teaching/Learning Project by President McCabe. Their charge is to create a list of issues that will need to be considered before formulating a plan for implementation. The groups vigorously attack the assignment, but it is difficult for them to find a beginning point for such a massive task.

During the report-out phase in the afternoon, it is apparent that there are issues common to all groups. Further, topics appear to cluster around the broad areas of college climate, teaching excellence, leadership, and institutional systems.

December through January 1986–1987

President McCabe and Project Director Mardee Jenrette visit each campus to exchange ideas with faculty and administrators, and to listen to questions and comments. A packet is mailed prior to the sessions to create a common ground for discussion. Materials include the original McCabe concept paper, *Organizing Miami-Dade Community College To Emphasize Faculty/Student Performance*, and the list of issues prepared after the "Conversation on teaching and learning" held in October (see Appendices A1,A16). Jenrette's cover memo alerts faculty and administrators to the upcoming series of meetings which will serve as a forum for the exchange of ideas. She urges, "With the project in its formative stage, now is the time for key issues to be exposed. When we begin to design the implementation phase, we will want to make sure to move in a meaningful direction."

A luncheon discussion with campus administrative leadership immediately precedes the open sessions: two, one-and-one-half hour meetings to which all faculty on the campus are invited. Two time periods increase the opportunity for faculty to attend.

Attendance is excellent (for example, on Medical Center Campus, with approximately 100 full-time faculty, 60 turn out). The presentation is met with hopeful enthusiasm and healthy skepticism. Faculty raise questions about how veterans will fit into the new program, whether or not their current academic rank and tenure will be grandfathered in, and how they can make their voices heard during the developmental phase of the project.

January 1987

On South Campus, the largest campus, members of the Project Steering Committee circulate a memo to all faculty and administrative colleagues indicating their availability at scheduled times and places. They write, "...(we) realize that we need your help and input. We further realize the need to keep you informed...(bring) us your questions, concerns and any information you think relevant to achieving the goals of this project."

January 1987

At one of its first meetings, the steering committee develops assumptions that establish an operational context for the project. These assumptions are: diversity is a key to teaching and learning at Miami-Dade and is to be valued; shared values concerning teaching and learning can be identified; behaviors that contribute to effective teaching and learning can be identified; the quality of educational programs and the teaching and learning environment can be enhanced by collaborative efforts of all college personnel; and there is continuing need for all college personnel to acquire knowledge and skills. The process of articulating these guidelines helps to bring the individual members of the steering committee together as a team and to link individual concepts of teaching/learning toward a common one.

May 1987

A *Teaching/Learning Project Bulletin* is published and distributed to all faculty and administrators. One semester has passed since the creation of the Steering Committee and initial four working subcommittees. The *Bulletin* urges participation and includes a response form with two questions:

1. What concerns do you have at this point in the development of the Teaching/Learning Project (about process or content)?

2. What suggestions do you have about effective ways to communicate the project's progress to you and your colleagues on an ongoing basis?

Twenty-four detailed responses are received. Most express concerns: How will this project affect promotions in the future? Is there a place in the project for librarians and other non-classroom faculty? When the project is done, will it really have made a difference in what happens in the classroom?

September 1987

The Steering Committee prepares a set of guidelines to govern subcommittee operations (see Appendix A15). Among the expectations they delineate are, "(identification of) the critical components of the issues to be addressed…(that) the matter will be well researched and adequate provision made for input and feedback from affected campus constituencies and experts."

At that same meeting the project goals are finalized:

1. To improve the quality of teaching and learning at Miami-Dade Community College.

2. To make teaching at Miami-Dade Community College a professionally rewarding career.

3. To make teaching and learning the focal point of college activities and decision- making processes.

September 1987

President McCabe hosts a luncheon for faculty members who have been with the college for more than twenty years. His letter of invitation says in part, "You have played an important role in making the college what it is today. I am soliciting your advice concerning our Teaching/Learning Project. Because of your knowledge and experience, I believe that you can provide particularly important insights" (see Appendix A13).

After the meal, three questions are discussed:

1. How can new faculty benefit from the rich experience of senior faculty?

2. What kind of institutional support through the years has been/would have been most beneficial in aiding you to fulfill your teaching role to the best of your ability?

3. What other advice would you give Miami-Dade Community College about its teaching/learning mission?

More than 100 veteran faculty attend. They generate a long list of ideas that will help project committee members develop recommendations. The feedback they offer indicates their pleasure at having been remembered and listened to in this way.

Critical Review

The process of selecting issues for the Miami-Dade Teaching/Learning Project was sound and comprised:

1. Advice from internal and external experts to identify issues that would be valid vis-a-vis the teaching/learning relationship and relevant in Miami-Dade's setting.

2. Considerable time in discussing the concept behind the project and soliciting ideas for the direction it should take. All faculty and academic administrators on all college campuses had the opportunity to attend group meetings with the president and project director.

3. Attention to group input. Ideas that surfaced in one meeting often formed the basis for discussion in subsequent ones. By providing documents prior to meetings and sharing products after meetings, consensus building was furthered.

4. The college president's leadership role. In every fact-finding meeting during the early stages of the project, the president showed his personal commitment and support and set a pattern that would be followed by every project committee: substantial input would be solicited before any recommendations would be made.

While the issues selected to pursue were correct, and great effort was expended to solicit input from faculty, hindsight suggests that we might have encouraged broader-based participation.

1. While attendance at meetings was good, significant numbers of faculty who did attend did not actively participate in discussion. While explanations are speculative, it is true that all meetings were planned for large groups, and many individuals are not comfortable speaking in an open forum. They might have shared their thoughts in a smaller group or in writing.

2. Opportunity for support staff to enter the process early in the project was not provided. Their perspective was thus missing from a number of recommendations put forward by project subcommittees.

3. While the student voice was represented through survey responses in a number of instances, student views did not shape the product of the "Conversation on teaching and learning." Whether there would have been substantive differences in the issues that emerged is, of course, speculative at this point.

Discussion

The teaching/learning relationship may be understood from at least three perspectives: the student, the teacher, and the institution. The student needs skills and competencies to ensure successful learning. The teacher must use effective strategies to help students learn. The institution should assess and advise students to place them in optimal settings, and it must support teachers in their work. Thus the teaching/learning relationship and the variables that affect it are complex, as are the issues that must be confronted to enhance that relationship.

There are neither universally correct issues to select as starting points nor universally correct final goals for a project. There are, however, locally appropriate ones. Selecting the issues you will address becomes a critically important task and suggests the need to incorporate research in the decision making process. Research in this context is defined in a broad way and encompasses interviews of individuals or groups, surveys with analysis of data returns, and literature searches. The need to implant a research component in a project begins with the selection of substantive issues to comprise the project agenda.

Employee Participation

Employees are an essential resource in helping to identify institutional teaching/learning issues. Involve the acknowledged leaders, both in the faculty and in the academic administration. But also include as many others who have a personal investment in the success of the institution as you can. Ask secretaries, who often have contact with students coming to departments for assistance, to participate. Ask counselors and advisors and ask the registrar and librarians to become involved. Also include the accountants and maintenance staff. Only a very narrow view of teaching and learning is limited to the teacher/student relationship. Other college personnel are often in a better position to see the influence of non-class-room/non-academic factors on student academic success. In short, try to involve all employees in identifying key institutional issues.

Student Involvement

Students should also be involved, but the significant question is, "What degree of involvement is practical?" Whether or not individual students can remain engaged over time is frequently a function of institutional type. In two-year commuter settings, for example, students are not likely to be able to be members of ongoing task groups. A workable alternative might be to sample the broader student population if and as appropriate.

Role of External Consultants

External consultants may also play a positive role in identifying key issues. They can enrich a project, but only when used for the correct purpose and at the correct time. Consultants can share with an institution the broad, national perspective on teaching and learning; they can help provide an overview and a sense of the issues that transcend a local scene. They can describe their experiences in similar settings, information that can be vital in helping a project move in a successful direction. If they spend enough time at your institution, they can provide observations and offer insights that those too involved with daily issues cannot have themselves. They can raise questions you would never think of or make an objective assessment of your subjective work.

What consultants cannot do is to provide definitive answers. They cannot tell you how what they have done or seen elsewhere will blend with your institutional culture. You must evaluate what they have done or seen. The initial phase of the project, then, is an ideal time to bring in outsiders if consultants are to be part of the overall plan. The beginning is the time to keep an open mind, for that is when the broadest range of possibilities exists and should be explored, when no judgments are yet needed on the feasibility of the directions to be pursued.

Consultants may provide an additional service as well. The participation of a well known expert, particularly one you can count on to deliver good work and who relates well to faculty, sends a signal that what is about to happen is important. This should advance your efforts to convince institutional personnel that a significant commitment to teaching and learning is being made through your project.

The Process of Identifying Issues

It is important to reach as many people as possible within the institution at an early stage. There will be a benefit beyond merely gathering information for decisions on the issues to pursue. Raising significant questions will stimulate people to think, to become interested, to interact with one another, and to take positions on teaching/learning issues. These experiences will prepare individuals to take active roles in the project at a later date.

In fact, a variety of strategies may be used to raise and refine local issues. Several are enumerated here. Each used alone has its strong and weak points; using a combination will increase the certainty that the issues being addressed are appropriate for your situation.

1. *Try several types of interactive techniques.* Bring faculty, staff, and administrators together to discuss teaching/learning as it applies to your institution. You can develop an entire discussion from one question: "From where you sit, what will it take to improve the institutional environment for teaching and learning?"

Adequate exploration of this question will require at least a half-day session. If faculty, staff, and administrators in your institution can speak freely with one another, it would be advantageous to create mixed groupings. If not, create groups in which members will feel comfortable to express their thoughts fully. Discussion groups should be limited to 15 individuals to permit each participant ample opportunity to speak. If you want to put the question to more people, convene more groups. The discussion locale should be removed from the work setting to minimize interruptions.

There is always the possibility that a discussion designed to elicit responses to questions that deal with improving teaching and learning will degenerate into a gripe session. It is important not to let that happen. While clearing the air is healthy, and some complaining should be permitted, cathartic sessions don't usually produce new directions. A strong discussion leader will be needed to phrase questions in positive terms and to help participants express themselves in positive ways. An effective leader will also be able to ensure that all suggestions are recorded in a non-evaluative manner. This may be the only time in the life of a project when it will be possible to explore possibilities without constraint. The opportunity should not be lost.

Focus interviewing is a variation on less structured, heterogeneous discussion groups. To create focus groups, turn to the representative bodies in your institution—the faculty senates, the administrative councils. But do not stop there. Target selected faculty—new to the institution, veterans of more than ten years—and selected administrators—academic deans, heads of support areas. Carefully selecting questions for focus groups and carefully selecting representative participants can greatly enrich the input you receive.

The focus technique should work well with students, too. In creating student groups be sure you sample from all those who will be affected by the outcome of the project.

As fruitful as discussions may be, they are inadequate to reach the objective of providing an opportunity to participate for everyone in the institution. It is not feasible to invite all personnel or large numbers of students to become members of a group, nor will all wish to be directly involved.

2. *Use surveys and questionnaires.* In our experience, surveys consisting of a set of carefully structured questions produced the greatest number of responses. Many people appreciate a topical trigger to stimulate their thinking. Outcomes of group discussion on improving teaching and learning become a good source of questions, so surveys that follow the discussion can build on those questions. Since as a discussion proceeds it is possible to prod and prompt to elicit more refined information, questions for a survey will have to be more carefully structured than those for a discussion or focus group. One cannot evaluate the quality or effectiveness of survey questions until the responses are received, when it is too late to make changes.

On the other hand, while a less structured instrument may yield fewer respondents, it provides an avenue for ideas broader than you might have generated from a set of structured questions. The purpose of your survey should guide the decisions you make on this matter.

It is important to distribute surveys to all personnel in your target group. This will at least ensure that everyone has had an opportunity to provide input. Mailings that go to home addresses often receive more attention and thus should increase the percentage of respondents. Weigh the cost of the mailing against your need for the information.

A most efficient way of getting large numbers of students to participate and to ensure that they have the time for in depth response is to reach them in class. Be sure to get a cross-section of the types of courses that the institution offers (e.g. technical, liberal arts) if the outcomes of your project are to affect students in all these areas. Enlist the help of faculty colleagues to distribute the surveys and to provide a rationale to students for the importance of the project and the need for the inclusion of a student voice.

In sum, providing opportunity does not guarantee a response, and surveys and questionnaires have their own set of limitations. There may be no representation from a segment of the population you specifically want to hear from, for instance. Further, responses may be ambiguous or overly abbreviated and there is no opportunity for the elaboration that results when there is discussion on the same topic. Surveying is most useful, then, as a back up to direct involvement through discussion. A combination of surveys and interviews would be most effective.

3. *Create a survey and send it to "sibling" institutions.* Ask what they see as the issues. (Define sibling as those having a similar service community.)

4. *Review institutional source documents.* Examine mission statements, annual goals and priorities, declarations made in course catalogs and in student and faculty handbooks. Documents prepared for or resulting from accreditation reviews can be especially fruitful resources.

A Clash of Issues

Because different constituencies of a college see the teaching/learning relationship from different perspectives, there may not be agreement on the priority that should be given to each of the issues raised. It will be the role of project leadership to set priorities, but there must be recognition that all the issues are important; each must be given a place in the project.

After exploring and assessing institutional practices, measuring your emerging list of concerns against a broader backdrop is one way to help set an order for addressing issues. While the body of literature continues to be updated, some references continue to be of great value. The following are illustrative.

1. Chickering, Arthur W. and Zelda F. Gamson. "Seven Principles for Good Practice in Undergraduate Education." *AAHE Bulletin*. Vol. 39(7) March 1987. The principles are expanded in "Applying the Seven Principles for Good Practice in Undergraduate Education." *New Directions for Teaching and Learning*, No. 47, Fall 1991, Jossey-Bass.The authors base their recommendations on 50 years of research on good teaching and learning in colleges and universities. They include discussions on contact between students and faculty, the use of active learning techniques, the giving of prompt feedback, and respecting diverse ways of learning.

2. Jossey-Bass paperback sourcebooks:
   New Directions for Higher Education
   New Directions for Teaching and Learning
   Jossey-Bass, Inc.
   433 California Street
   San Francisco, CA 94104

3. Educational Resources Information Center (ERIC). The ERIC data base includes *Resources in Education* (RIE) and *Current Index to Journals in Education* (CIJE).

   Office of Educational Research and Improvement (OERI)
   U.S. Department of Education
   Washington, DC 20208

Clarity of Issue Definition

It is important to start out with a clear sense of direction. On the other hand, it is just as important to acknowledge that this project will unfold as you go, and thus your initial concept may turn out to be incomplete. As you initiate the process, keep these general principles in mind:

1. Each issue chosen must be seen as relevant; it must be important to the various constituencies of the institution. This helps make your teaching/learning project a force that unites faculty, staff, and administrators rather than one that divides them.

2. The selected issues must be able to be controlled by your institution, and thus be supportable by its resources. If the base to support potential outcomes does not exist, then the creation of that base must become part of the project.

3. While issues must be well defined for a clear action plan to develop, expect that you will be refining the scope as the project unfolds. Be clear, but stay flexible.

A good idea might be to carefully define a few starting points and leave what will come next sketchy. Individuals who enter the project at a later date will be able to contribute to the necessary refinement of issues, broadening the base of ownership within the institution and strengthening the final product.

ORGANIZING
AND EXECUTING

The issues may be right. The timing may be right. The level of commitment from key individuals may be there. Still the project cannot succeed unless it is organized well. At this stage you must think about: who will be in charge; who will do the work; how the work will be done; how individuals will participate directly in the project; how those who are not directly involved will be able to critique what is being done; and how recommendations will be adopted. A consideration of the foregoing issues will begin in this chapter and continue in Chapters 5, 6, and 7.

Notes from the Miami-Dade Diary

September 1986

At the same time a college-wide committee is screening candidates for project director, a process begins to appoint members to a college-wide Teaching/Learning Project Steering Committee to be comprised of twenty-four individuals: seventeen faculty members; the four campus academic deans; the dean of institutional research; the district vice president for education, and President McCabe. The selection proceeds according to Policy I-80, the Governance Constitution of the Faculty Senates, which addresses college-wide committees in the following manner: "All task forces dealing with college-wide issues shall be appointed by the college president in consultation with the president of the (faculty senates) consortium. The membership of the task forces shall be selected from a list of individuals nominated...jointly by the campus vice president and the faculty senate president. Balancing factors must be considered in composition of committees, and the list of nominees will be greater than the number to be selected in order that these factors may be considered." The process moves slowly, but it moves.

November 1986

The first Teaching/Learning Project Steering Committee meeting is held even though all appointments have not yet been made. After introductions it is noted that collectively nearly 400 years of service to Miami-Dade is represented by those present. The roles and responsibilities of the Steering Committee and the project director are delineated (see Appendix A3).

December 1986

The college president decides to pay a stipend to faculty working on the project. He listens to arguments put forward by the Steering Committee that it is time, more than money, that is needed to do the job. He approves, instead, one class-equivalent in released time for each faculty member on the project.

January 1987

At the second Steering Committee meeting, the project director presents issues that the project might address. These issues were derived from the day-long discussion on teaching and learning held in October. They are: student learning outcomes; characteristics of an effective learning environment; effective teacher behaviors; getting feedback on teaching; a formal evaluation system that will differentiate unacceptable/good/excellent teaching; tenure/promotion decisions based on congruence with college valued outcomes; new and part-time faculty hiring and integration; support for faculty; administrative leadership to support teaching; endowed teaching chairs; and the role of non-teaching units in teaching and learning (see Appendix A16). The discussion produces an order in which to address the issues and "idea teams" to do the actual work of the project.

February 1987

By the third meeting, the concept of "idea teams" as the work vehicle of the project takes shape. The teams will be sub-committees of the Steering Committee. Each Steering Committee member will serve on one of the four subcommittees that have been designated to start the project: Teaching/Learning Values, New Faculty, Teaching/Learning Environment, and Faculty Behavior. Membership will expand beyond the Steering Committee. Additional members will be selected by the process specified in I-80 and criteria for subcommittee nominees will include expertise on the issue, campus representation, interest in the topic, and special group membership. A sub-committee will be appointed at the point in the project when it is most appropriate to address the issue. The length of the appointment will be determined by the nature of the task. A faculty member from the Steering Committee will chair each sub-committee. Each subcommittee receives a general charge that focuses on preliminary planning issues including: defining tasks; selecting a chair; identifying data sources relevant to the completion of tasks; establishing data collection strategies; setting time frames and milestones; estimating budget needs; and planning communication strategies that will provide for involvement and buy-in by Miami-Dade personnel. Each sub-committee will carefully research its subject and provide for input and feedback from experts and affected constituencies (see Appendix A15). The end product of each subcommittee will be a series of recommendations for action that will be made to the project Steering Committee.

Operating rules are formulated. The Steering Committee will meet once per month during fall and winter (i.e. major) semesters at a standard time so that teachers can arrange schedules. Lunch will be served at the start of each meeting to save time and to accommodate the needs of those traveling from other campuses. The Steering Committee will not hold regular meetings during spring/summer when many faculty are on leave. Subcommittee chairs will give progress reports at each

Steering Committee meeting. Subcommittee members who are not on the Steering Committee are welcome to attend the monthly meetings. The Steering Committee will give feedback to subcommittees and will accept or reject all recommendations.

Equipped with a set of project assumptions, goals, and a charge, the four subcommittees go to work. The Faculty Behaviors Subcommittee, concerned about the term "behavior," renames itself the Faculty Excellence Subcommittee and refines its purpose: to describe and get consensus on a core of fundamental qualities and characteristics which constitute excellence in faculty members involved in the teaching/learning process at Miami-Dade Community College. The membership of the subcommittee consists of four faculty from the Steering Committee, two administrators from the Steering Committee (one academic dean and the dean of institutional research) and four additional faculty selected through the I-80 process. All campuses are represented. Disciplines encompass technical areas, arts and humanities, sciences, and physical education. The membership includes men and women, African Americans, Anglos and Hispanics.

March 1987

After some false starts and struggles to grasp viable approaches to the charge, the Faculty Excellence Subcommittee decides to create a survey based on research on effective teaching, learning principles and styles, and learning assessment. The subcommittee also articulates three beliefs from which it will proceed: 1) all dedicated professors are committed to excellence—excellence in teaching to achieve excellence in student learning; 2) the achievement of individual excellence at Miami-Dade Community College will be, to a large extent, the result of collegial effort; and 3) while each faculty member is unique and diversity is valued, a core of specific behaviors that contribute to effective teaching and learning can be identified.

April 1987

The Faculty Excellence Subcommittee presents to the Steering Committee thirteen principles of learning on which its survey instrument will be based (see Appendix B1). The survey instrument will have fifty-three items and will be field tested with small groups of faculty and administrators in the spring and summer terms (see Appendix B2).

July 1987

College-wide, 120 faculty and administrators volunteer to meet in small group sessions with the Faculty Excellence Subcommittee. They complete the survey with a team of subcommittee members and then participate in a verbal critique and discussion about the subcommittee's charge and approach to the task. Response to the survey is not what was expected; the feedback on the list of items is generally negative. But the subcommittee receives valuable information. They learn that some items were so specific that many faculty felt them to be unnecessarily constraining and that others were too ambiguous to be of value. In addition, there was not a good fit for non-teaching faculty and there was too much redundancy. The subcommittee concludes that the format it has chosen for input is basically a good one; it decides to shorten and revise the survey and try again in the fall term.

September through October 1987

A second draft of the excellence survey is prepared, and a second small-group field test is carried out. Although the response is more positive this time, revisions follow. The third draft, a twenty-eight item survey, is sent through inter-office mail to all faculty, all administrators, and a sampling of students in classes (see Appendix B3). Thirty-five percent of administrators and 40% of faculty respond. There is strong support for all twenty-eight items. Analysis reveals that "knowledgeable about work" is rated highest by all three groups and that five of the highest-scoring seven items fall under the general heading of interpersonal skills.

January 1988

The Subcommittee on Faculty Excellence presents a draft report to the Steering Committee. The subcommittee has organized its findings on qualities and characteristics of excellent faculty according to a scheme used by Roueche and Baker in their study of Miami-Dade: motivation, interpersonal skills, and intellectual skills. The twenty-eight qualities are identified and

elaborated in a narrative format. The Steering Committee
moves to create a document that will be taken to a larger audience for discussion.

February 1988

A *T/L Bulletin* is sent to all employees to report the progress
of the Faculty Excellence Subcommittee, to alert readers that
there will be a retreat in the next month to discuss the draft
Statement of Faculty Excellence and related matters, and to invite
readers to contact retreat participants (listed in the *Bulletin*) with
any concerns they would like to see raised at the retreat.

March 1988

The Statement of Faculty Excellence, Draft #2, produced after
the February Steering Committee meeting, is taken to an off-
campus, two-day retreat, which seventy-four college faculty
and administrators attend (see Appendix A14). Attendees represent the Teaching/Learning Steering Committee, the Faculty
Excellence Subcommittee, and the College President's Council.
Also participating are external consultants: Sandra Acebo (Los
Medanos Community College, California), Nancy Armes (Dallas Community College, Texas), George Baker (University of
Texas, Austin), Russell Edgerton (American Association of
Higher Education), Michael Hooks (Valencia Community Col-
lege, Florida), Terry O'Banion (League for Innovation in the
Community College), Dick Richardson (Arizona State Univer-
sity), and John Roueche (University of Texas, Austin).

Statement of Faculty Excellence, Draft #3 emerges from the
retreat discussion. New features include: dividing the section
"Intellectual Skills" into two, Knowledge Base and Application
of Knowledge Base; a slight rewording of some qualities, principally to broaden their applicability (for example changing
"student" to "individual" as in, "treats all *individuals* with
respect"); the addition of a twenty-ninth characteristic, "knowledgeable about how students learn." "Displays a genuine sense
of humor conducive to a positive teacher/student relationship"
becomes, "creates a climate that is conducive to learning." This
change is the most difficult to effect, with the discussion becoming quite testy at times. Not much humor is in evidence as
humor is discussed.

April 1988

The president sends the *Statement of Faculty Excellence* Draft #3 to all faculty and professional staff. His cover memo tells them that he is allowing time for these important contents to be absorbed. Formal feedback will not be requested until the following fall.

September through October 1988

McCabe holds small group meetings and invites written responses on Draft #3. This will be the last opportunity to provide input to the *Statement of Faculty Excellence.*

October 1988

The *Statement of Faculty Excellence,* in its fourth draft, is adopted by the College President's Council and the District Board of Trustees (see Appendix B4).

Critical Review

The initial organization of the project and its execution are responsible in large part for successful progress. There were, of course, some decisions that were better than others. Clearly some of the good decisions kept the more questionable ones from having serious consequences.

Among positive practices worth highlighting are:

1. Using established college policy and procedure to select the project director and to make committee appointments. The processes were time consuming and often seemed tedious to those anxious to begin an activity, but the approach proved worthwhile. A strong faculty voice was assured in what was clearly going to be a project that would have great impact on the faculty. From the beginning, the faculty senates used their position in the formal process to nominate faculty who had a history of strong faculty advocacy and who would be able to stand up to administrators if necessary. In later project years, these "watch dogs" had the necessary credibility with their colleagues to say, "This project is legitimate; pay attention; participate because the outcomes will affect you."

2. Delineating roles of project personnel immediately. For

example, it was quickly established that the Steering Committee members would assess needs of their Miami-Dade constituency, recommend and approve project activities, review and monitor progress, act on recommendations, and advocate the project. At the same time, the project director would facilitate the work of the Steering Committee, assist subcommittees, and prepare proposals and reports. Productive working relationships resulted.

3. Establishing subcommittees early in the project and tying them tightly to the Steering Committee. Getting quickly beyond talking about teaching and learning to acting on important teaching/learning issues created a momentum that was critical to moving through later difficult periods. The strategy permitted the work to be done by task groups of manageable size (under twenty); at the same time it allowed over 200 individuals to participate in the project. Steering Committee members advanced from one subcommittee to the next as tasks were completed. New members could be appointed as new subcommittees were formed, and continuity could be preserved without sacrificing the benefits that come from fresh ideas and viewpoints.

4. Insisting that faculty chair subcommittees. Non-participating faculty throughout the institution, even if far removed from direct knowledge of the project, knew that faculty were taking charge of what was certain to have great impact on the faculty role at the college. The practice additionally encouraged greater commitment from faculty members on subcommittees. In the one instance where an administrator took charge, faculty participation declined.

5. Starting with the particular four subcommittees previously mentioned. The issues those subcommittees addressed helped lay a firm foundation for later subcommittee work. They did not delve into threatening areas, and they made recommendations that would call for more support for faculty rather than more work from them. The project was helped to a smooth start and would have a history of success to fall back on as the more sensitive issues of evaluation and the awarding of promotion, tenure, and endowed chairs were brought forward.

6. Devoting time to input and feedback as subcommittee tasks unfolded. It was frustrating to watch the weeks and sometimes months roll by as people reviewed, critiqued, and then returned their comments. The volume of response created the problem of determining what commentary was valid, i.e. what was representative of a significant segment of the college community. Despite the drawbacks, the time and the process were critical to a project whose success would be measured by institutional buy-in. For instance, by the time the Faculty Excellence Subcommittee released its third-draft, twenty-eight item survey, broad based institutional support was nearly guaranteed. Even after extensive participation, more input was sought at the retreat on faculty excellence, and the *Statement of Faculty Excellence* that emerged was stronger because of that decision.

7. Taking care to experiment during minor semesters, but to do anything of consequence only when faculty would be present in large numbers. Even if it meant a delay of several months, making major decisions affecting faculty when they would not be present to participate in the process would have been a serious violation of trust.

8. Paying participants with released time as the preferred option. Individuals were given the time to devote adequate attention to the project, and they clearly understood that the project was of great importance to the college. Additionally, major meetings like the retreat were conducted during the work week, further reinforcing the message of importance.

There was, of course, room for improvement in the way the project was organized and executed:

1. Failure to define clearly enough a profile of the ideal nominee for each subcommittee as it was created. On occasion the resulting pool of nominees was too weak to use, some ill will was created, and some time was wasted.

2. Failure to consistently provide subcommittees adequate training or monitoring. While all issues were complex and needed much time to address properly, some project subcommittees took unnecessarily long because they had false

starts or because they began to develop recommendations that could not be supported. Problems could be traced to poor organizational or research skills, or lack of prescriptive directions. Later subcommittees, in part because of greater intervention by the project director or assigned consultants, profited from the experiences of earlier ones.

3. Inadequate staff support to the project. Dedicated secretarial/clerical personnel is necessary to maintain budgets, produce reports in a timely fashion, and keep channels of communication open.

4. Failure to appoint the project director to the President's Council, the principal governing body of the college. The President's Council frequently makes decisions that affect teaching/learning; a number were not transmitted to the project in time to strengthen work in progress. (This situation became more of a problem during the implementation phase of the project. Elaboration will be found in Chapters 6 and 7.)

5. Failure to convince sizeable segments of the institution that there would be later consequences if they did not respond to invitations to give input or feedback. As much as participation was encouraged, and although 300 to 400 responses would be received to each faculty excellence survey, the numbers represent only 35%–40% of Miami-Dade faculty and administrators. Response rates to requests by other subcommittees were similar. The Steering Committee's roles as project advocate and information-conduit were underplayed, and the power of one-to-one contact with colleagues was not adequately exploited. The negative consequences materialized during the implementation phase of the project when, "Where did this come from? I never saw it," were heard.

6. Failure to distinguish real issues from distractors. For example, that non-classroom faculty (counselors and librarians) were not adequately represented in the *Statement of Faculty Excellence* was a repeated charge. Even though modifications to the document were made, and even though the *Statement* had already been formally adopted by the Board

of Trustees in 1988, the charge persisted until a Non-Classroom Faculty Subcommittee was created in 1989 to review the *Statement* and recommend necessary modifications to make it applicable to all faculty. The outcome of that subcommittee's work was interesting. While some of the language in the narrative was made more general, the subcommittee determined that each of the original 29 qualities did apply to non-classroom faculty. The lesson learned at Miami-Dade was that if teaching/learning is to be everyone's responsibility, *everyone* must be invited into the project.

7. Failure to provide for initial support staff representation on the Steering Committee. The rationale for inclusion can be derived from the preceding paragraph. Although the problem was rectified, the consequences of earlier exclusion created unnecessary and persistent difficulties in working with that constituency.

Discussion

Project Management

It is important to establish at the outset who will be in charge of the project. One individual should serve as project director. Someone must feel a personal responsibility for keeping the project going. Whether the director's appointment is full time should be dictated by the scope and complexity of the project as defined. Whatever the case, there should be the expectation that directing this project will require a significant percentage of professional time. It must not be, "something to do if time permits." To expand representation in managing the project, an advisory board can be appointed to work closely with the project director.

Most institutions rely heavily on committees as a vehicle to carry out the work of a project. There may be a temptation to assign managerial responsibilities to a committee as well, since committees do expand the opportunity for participation. The negative aspects of using a committee in a long-term project, however, outweigh the positive aspects. Putting a committee in charge effectively means no one is in charge. Discrete tasks can be assigned and discrete topics can be covered at committee meetings, but there are day-to-day details of running a project which require immediate attention, and committee members are not always available. Someone must have the project overview, and institutional personnel need to have a number they can call and a face they can associate with providing answers when help is needed. Furthermore, the project will probably take a long time, and a commitment must be made for the long term. Committee assignments are often one-term or one-year obligations. It is disruptive to have no project "memory" or continuity. Committees, then, should do the substantive work, but should not be in charge of managing the project.

Task Management

A follow-up question to, "Who should be in charge?" is, "Who should do the work?" The answer depends on the type of work to be done. Here are some guidelines:

1. The phases of the project that deal with appointing individuals to work on the project and adopting recommendations should be assigned to appropriate existing institutional bodies like faculty senates, executive committees, and boards of trustees.

2. The phases of the project that deal with coordinating efforts and individuals, facilitating, coaching and monitoring, keeping records, managing budget and paper flow, and other managerial details should be attended to by the project director.

3. The phases of the project that will address time lines and flow of activities, adding new issues to the agenda or modifying the direction of existing ones, and taking preliminary action on recommendations should be assigned to an advisory board working in conjunction with the project director.

4. The phases of the project that involve researching topics and making recommendations should be given to task forces or committees.

5. When recommendations are finally adopted, phasing changes into the organizational routine should be delegated to those who administer the areas in which the changes will fall.

Processes for Obtaining Involvement

How should individuals become involved in the project? Individuals can volunteer, they can be appointed or elected, or a combination of selection mechanisms may be used. There are advantages and disadvantages to each method depending on a number of factors, including the tasks individuals are to accomplish.

If it is important to have specific roles represented or specific individuals directly participating, then assigning personnel to work on the project best meets those objectives. Appointing the project director assures the CEO that he/she will be working with an individual with whom he/she feels comfortable. On the negative side, this closed, controlled process may create resentment. The appropriateness of the choice may not be as apparent to others as it is to the CEO. A low level of discontent that develops early in a long-term project can grow into a very serious problem. Furthermore, an appointee may not be interested in the position and thus may lack the motivation needed for the success of the project, may make no substantive contribution, and may even impede progress.

Staffing committees and other task groups with volunteers may initially appear to be an attractive alternative. This process insures participants will be motivated and fosters in the institution at large the sense that the decision to get involved rests with individuals. But there are drawbacks. Must all who volunteer be taken? What if the numbers are too large to be effective? What if the critical expertise or skills are not present within the group of volunteers? What if volunteers are not respected by their colleagues? Remember, you are always sending messages about the project and its status. The people involved in the project reflect the project's importance to the institution. What if the individuals who comprise the volunteer pool do not reflect their constituency by race, ethnic, gender, professional profile, or other characteristics you think are important to have represented in the project's work force?

Electing individuals may address some of the weaknesses of both volunteering and appointing while retaining the advantage of staffing through a participative process. First, this process encourages individuals to volunteer, yet does not guarantee their involvement. Second, elected individuals should have the support of the constituency that elected them. Drawbacks do remain, however. If a balance of skills, areas represented, or even gender or ethnic considerations are important, then an election is too open a process. The more tightly structured the process is, the closer one can get to a balance in make up.

Here, then, are some suggestions to minimize the drawbacks discussed:

1. Call for volunteers, but do not create an expectation that all who volunteer will be selected (see Appendix A18). Carefully delineate both the characteristics and skills needed in participants and the commitments that are expected of those who serve. Then make appointments from the pool of volunteers.

2. Hold elections, but establish eligibility requirements for those who would run. Base the requirements on project needs (e.g. is it important that faculty be tenured? that administrators be from academic areas?) Hold elections by area to assure representation from those that are vital to the project (e.g. not just representatives from liberal arts faculty, but science, communications, humanities, etc.).

3. Combine elements of volunteerism and appointment. Call for volunteers. Clearly explain what is needed, that all who volunteer will not be selected, and that other individuals may be appointed to fill in representational deficiencies. Ensure that actual appointments are made by the joint effort of several individuals who represent the various institutional constituencies that you see as key to the success of the project.

4. Establish a committee to make final appointments, no matter how the pool of potential appointees has been created. Give the committee the power to make the decisions or charge it to recommend appropriate individuals.

Using Committees Effectively

Any project intended to have major institutional impact should be worked on by committees if for no other reason than to increase the number of people who can play direct roles.

There are a number of factors that contribute to making committees function well or poorly. The critical decision points begin with the method chosen to select project participants, and continue with the decisions made about constituencies to be represented, with the manner in which committees will be charged and trained, with the way committee work will be monitored and supported, with the decision whether or not to compensate members, with the size of the committee, with clarification of the committee's tasks, the committee's leader, and the person to whom they will report. Planning for all these factors will help determine how well your committees work. While there are not universally correct responses, answers are needed and the questions should be thought through, alternatives weighed, and decisions communicated before problems develop.

Here are important questions to consider about task forces/committees:

1. What will they do? The task forces/committees you appoint will be most successful if each is charged to explore one specific aspect of your teaching/learning project. The issues must be clearly articulated, the parameters for the committees' operations clear, and time lines to reach objectives and support for undertakings spelled out. The clearer the charge, the better committees will function. This is an example of a clear charge.

   Charge to the College-Wide Committee on Chairpersons Support/Compensation

   The committee is charged with three responsibilities:

   - *to delineate the responsibilities that have caused an increased chair work load as a result of the impending implementation of faculty advancement policies and procedures*

   - *to review and delineate the range of compensation (release time, supplements, other) that currently exists throughout the college*

   - *to recommend specific compensation/support/training that will make the chair role "doable."*

   - *Time frame: fall term, 1991*

2. How will members be compensated? Consider this one carefully. Assignments given to individuals who already have full work lives often receive inadequate attention. If task force members will be asked to dedicate significant amounts of time to the project, and if you wish to take the opportunity to send a strong message that the outcomes of this project are vital to the institution, then compensate participants. Released time is ideal since it says to individuals that this task is part of an obligation to the institution, as important as others for which they are compensated. If this is not possible, some form of overload should be considered. Use whatever is traditional in your system.

   The decision to compensate should not be made lightly, nor should it be made without consideration of the financial resources that have been set aside to support the project. Personnel will probably be the most costly budget item. If you plan to compensate, be clear about what level of direct involvement will trigger compensation. Make the decision, communicate it, and adhere to it. Fairness and equity issues are frequently the basis of problems and can be easily avoided.

3. What should the composition of the task force be? Let the specific task and some general principles guide your response to this question. Those who will be principally affected by the outcome of task force work should make up the majority of the membership. For example: if the recommendations will focus on teaching strategies, teaching faculty should dominate; if the charge centers on administrative support for teaching and learning, more administrators should be on the committee.

   No task force should be comprised solely of the affected constituency. Any set of recommendations, even if it appears only classrooms will be affected, will ripple to others. These others should be represented. Remember the principle that teaching and learning improvement is the responsibility of all individuals within the institution. The composition of a working group helps to broadcast that message and to unify various constituencies of the college.

In addition, it is often difficult for those responsible for maintaining an operation to make recommendations that will directly affect their own work. While their expertise is certainly vital to the committees' investigations, the naive outsider is essential for creative solutions to problems.

It is not necessary for every task force member to have voting power. For example, if a group is expecting to survey heavily within the institution, it may wish to call upon the services of institutional research. If it is exploring the possibility of changing the formal reward systems of the institution, it may wish to hear from the personnel department. Individuals can be brought in as resources on an as-needed basis; they do not necessarily need to be full members of the committee itself. For example:

Composition of the College-Wide Chairpersons Support/ Compensation Committee: 2 faculty; 8 chairpersons; 2 associate deans; 2 deans; 2 non-voting consultants (financial officer and chair of faculty advancement policy committee).

4. What is the ideal size of a task force? There is a balance required here between trying to assure adequate representation and creating a body that can function effectively. In any meeting, it is difficult for individuals to participate fully in a group that has more than fifteen members. If the task force must be larger because of other considerations, then it might subdivide for specific tasks and reconvene for feedback, input, and decision-making sessions.

5. How should committees be charged and trained? The members of a committee should receive a written letter of appointment and should be charged at their first meeting. Every effort should be made to ensure that all members of the committee can be present so that the instructions are heard without the need for later reinterpretation. If possible, the CEO should deliver the charge or at least emphasize his/her support and interest in the work about to be undertaken. The charge should be delivered orally and in writing.

You will need to gauge how many of the members of the task force have had substantial committee experience. If many have not, initial guidance will help task force members through a period that can be frustrating and disheartening. Suggest they select their next meeting time before they leave that day. Suggest they elect a chair before they adjourn. Explain what resources are available to support their work (clerical, duplicating, money to bring in consultants or to make site visits to other institutions) and what is expected of them in terms of keeping of minutes, reporting progress, and completing tasks. Any other expectations should be communicated as well: Must they do research before making recommendations? Will they be preparing a formal final report?

Be sensitive to the differences in task forces on which faculty, administrators, or staff predominate. Administrators as a group probably will have had the most experience with working on tasks where the goal is given but the route must be planned. They also will have the greatest familiarity with doing work through committees. Faculty are most used to making decisions for and about things that affect them directly. When they work collaboratively, it is almost always with a few peers, and those colleagues are usually from their own disciplines. Support staff probably will have had the least experience in a task of this nature. They will need the most assistance to become full participants in the teaching/learning project.

6. Who should chair a task force? One can hope that someone with leadership skills and the desire to lead will be selected, but this will not always be the case when a committee selects its own leader. Often the selection process is uncomfortable for the newly charged committee. Individuals may not know each other well, and the first person to volunteer may go unchallenged. You can circumvent this problem by appointing a chair. You will have to decide if that action will have negative consequences in your institution. Even if the committee makes the decision, you should insist that the chair be someone from the majority constituency of the committee. For instance, if the committee is addressing a faculty issue, the chair should be a faculty member. Later

on, as the task force begins making its recommendations, the chances that those principally affected will be favorably disposed to those recommendations will increase if the committee chair is one of their own colleagues.

It will be up to the project director to gauge the leadership skills of the chair and thus to determine how much guidance that individual will need. It is very gratifying to see individuals grow in the chair role as time passes. However, professional growth is neither automatic nor necessarily an objective for the task force. If the charge is clear and if appropriate support is given, a positive outcome is more likely.

7. How should task force work be monitored, and how should the progress of task forces be coordinated? If you have decided to appoint an advisory group or steering committee, its members can play a significant role in these processes. If advisory board members serve on task forces, they can report the progress of the task force to the board and additionally report back to the task force information about other groups working on related recommendations. For more consistent and closer monitoring, the project director should play a role. A clear reporting relationship should be established between the project director and the chair of the task force. The chair should be expected to consult the project director when help or advice is needed. He/she should be expected to alert the project director when recommendations are forthcoming or problems of significance are developing. The project director will be able to judge from minutes and other less formal contact whether or not progress is satisfactory, where clarification of the charge might be called for, what additional resources might be necessary to help the group function, and how else to facilitate the process.

The project director should not plan to attend each meeting of the task force. First, if a number of committees are operating concurrently, the project director would be unable to meet this objective. Second, the constant presence of the project director might have an inhibiting effect on the day-to-day workings of the committee. The members should feel that they can explore any issue without having their preliminary ideas or opinions subjected to outside scrutiny. No matter how unobtrusive the project director, he/she will never be perceived as a colleague of equal status in the group.

8. What should task forces be asked to produce as a final product? The task force should be asked for a final report that chronicles the process it followed to complete its task, a final set of recommendations, and the bases for those recommendations. It is not wise to ask a task force in most cases to recommend *how* something should occur; rather it should be describing *what* needs to happen. An exception may be made to this rule if the task force members are actually those individuals who will have to implement the recommendations. For instance, a task force of faculty and academic administrators might recommend that feedback be given by students to all faculty. They can specify at what point in a term, how often, what type of instrument should be used, and who will see the feedback reports. Details like who will process the forms, how they will be stored prior to processing, and how much computer time will be dedicated to the project should be left to appropriate professionals.

The Scope of Involvement

You should try to have as many people as possible directly involved. There is no better way to feel like the owner of a project than to be one of its creators. To the degree that this is not possible, everyone in the institution, no matter its size, should have the sense that they can participate in some fashion. This does not necessarily mean that everyone can directly serve, but all should have the opportunity to provide input and give feedback before decisions are made. Keeping people informed (more about this in the next chapter) and providing ample opportunity for input and feedback will be invaluable as you approach the point where individuals will need to alter their behavior to accommodate the changes that the project will indeed make.

The desire to participate usually builds as the project progresses. Those more cautious individuals who have held back will become interested in getting directly involved as they begin to see results. There should always be opportunity to increase membership; the task force is an excellent vehicle.

COMMUNICATING

E ffective communication with institutional constituents and the ultimate success of an institution-wide effort are closely related. Decisions about how, how often, and with whom to communicate should be made early in the life of a project. Readers should keep in mind when evaluating the material in this chapter that Miami-Dade is a five-campus urban college serving close to 80,000 credit-students annually. The communications network required may be quite different at a single-campus college with 1,000 students.

Notes from the Miami-Dade Diary

June 1986

A format is initiated through which key individuals can come together to interact over an issue of importance. The site is away from distractions of the daily work environment. Food is served, and there is sufficient time allotted for meaningful interchange of ideas. In this first instance, the participants are 120 administrative and faculty leaders. They are invited by the college president to hear his thoughts on improving teaching and learning at the college.

Through the years the same vehicle is used intermittently.

1) In October of the same year the day-long, on-campus "conversation on teaching and learning" serves as a brainstorming session through which initial directions and key issues for the project are selected by twenty-five faculty and administrators and five external consultants. 2) In June 1987 President McCabe hosts a breakfast meeting of administrators at a local hotel; he uses the occasion to reiterate his commitment to the six-month-old project and to communicate his expectation of their support as well. 3) In September 1987 senior faculty (those with more than twenty years' tenure) are invited by McCabe to an off-campus luncheon. He thanks them for their service to the college and invites them to help set direction for the project (see Appendix A13). 4) In October 1988 there is another off-campus luncheon for the first group of faculty to serve as mentors to new faculty. Deans and campus presidents are present as well. McCabe thanks them and uses the opportunity to reemphasize the purpose of the mentor program and the larger goals of the project. 5) In March 1990 participants in a "ten/ten" meeting (ten faculty senators, ten deans and campus presidents) spend an afternoon with the Faculty Advancement Procedures Committee, giving feedback on draft proposals for performance review, tenure and promotions decisions, performance portfolios, and endowed chairs. 6) As we complete this diary entry in June 1993, 108 faculty and administrators are preparing for a full-day meeting during which proposed changes to the faculty advancement processes will be debated.

September 1986

Communication about the project outside the college begins with the publication of *Taking Teaching Seriously*, an interview with McCabe in *AAHE Bulletin 39 (1)*. In that same month the *Miami News* publishes, "M-DCC plans to reward top teachers." Articles follow in the *Chronicle of Higher Education, The Teaching Professor, Higher Education and National Affairs, Community College Week* and more. By February 1988 visits of representatives from colleges and universities across the country begin.

October 1986

The first *Teaching/Learning Project Bulletin* introduces the project director and lists the participants in the "conversation on teaching and learning" held earlier in the month (see Appendix A2). Readers are invited to call them for more information. The *Bulletin* is printed on goldenrod paper, one that has not been widely used previously for duplicating. With time, it becomes readily identifiable as a message-carrier from the project.

For the term of the project, the *Bulletin* will be used to: 1) publish the charge of new subcommittees and introduce their members (see Appendix A17); 2) provide updates including invitations to comment and become involved in tasks in progress; 3) report on the disposition of recommendations as they are finalized. The *Bulletin* is produced as needed and the number varies each year; the average is twelve. Frequency of publication parallels activity of the academic calendar; few appear during the May-through-August period.

December 1986 through January 1987

McCabe holds a series of short meetings on each campus to introduce the teaching/learning concept and preliminary thinking on components of the project. Comments are solicited. He will make the rounds again as the focus turns from articulating qualities of faculty excellence to specifying policies and procedures for faculty advancement.

January 1987

Electronic communication begins. Voice mail is installed on all Steering Committee members' telephones, and a distribution group is created to interconnect them. This becomes a major means to provide or request information in a short turn-around time.

Informational videotapes are produced and copies are sent to all campuses. When most timely for the topic, they are played continuously in high traffic areas (building atria, faculty senate offices). The first, in November 1987, records a question and answer session held between the college president and faculty senators on the endowed chair program. A September 1988 tape features members of the Faculty Advancement Subcommittee talking about the work they will be doing on performance review, promotion, tenure, and endowed teaching chair policies. Still later, in February and October of 1992 and February of 1993, videos are made of training sessions for promotions, promotions appeals, and endowed chair decision-making committees. Campus centers for teaching and learning have copies that are intended for viewing by committee members who miss training. As is true with all other project videotapes, these are also made available to others who express interest in viewing them.

May 1987

Reporting begins to key institutional bodies. The Board of Trustees is informed of principal project goals, project background and objectives, procedures/products, and status of the first four subcommittees. Future plans are communicated as well: to change promotion and tenure policies; to focus on the ways teachers can get feedback; to implement the endowed chair program; to provide for participation beyond the Steering Committee and its subcommittees; to interact with external consultants; and to link with other institutions having similar teaching/learning goals. In December 1987 the final report of the first subcommittee to complete its charge, the Values Subcommittee, is presented to the Board for discussion and review. This practice will be repeated for all subsequent subcommittees.

In October 1987 the first overview is presented at the fall workshop of the combined faculty senates. Thereafter the project is given time on the agenda of each fall and spring workshop. The initial presentation is made by McCabe; however, subsequent reports are given by the project director and/or chairs of project subcommittees. Reports at monthly campus faculty senate meetings or college-wide senate consortium meetings are irregular, rare, and made only upon request of these bodies.

In March 1988 the project director provides the first update to the members of the President's Council, the decision-making body of the college. Membership includes the college president, the five campus presidents, the five district vice presidents, the faculty senates consortium president, the five campus faculty senate presidents, and (as of January 1991) the five campus support staff council presidents. The project will become an increasingly frequent item on the President's Council agenda through the years, and the project director becomes a frequent guest at meetings. Presentation topics include final subcommittee reports and recommendations for adoption by the council, updates on progress, and resolutions from the Steering Committee.

May 1987

Existing college publications become vehicles to disseminate information. *Information in Brief* is McCabe's one-page newsletter to all personnel. The May issue features a detailed progress report. *Insight*, the Miami-Dade house magazine, periodically reports on the project. In September 1987 Pat Cross's three-month residency is highlighted, in December 1987 subcommittee progress is detailed, and in June 1992 the first twenty-five endowed chair recipients are profiled. Student newspapers on all campuses report on aspects that will be of particular interest to students: the college-wide student feedback program; teachers going back to school (i.e. the graduate courses on teaching and learning); and the endowed chair program.

May 1987

Communication through surveys begins. *Teaching/Learning Bulletin 1(6)* asks three questions: Are there any concerns you have at this point about the project (now in its sixth month)? Do you have suggestions for effective communication strategies? Do you have any other comments? Each subcommittee uses surveying as a strategy to communicate with constituents (see Appendix C1).

August 1987

The project becomes a regular feature on the agenda for the new faculty pre-service orientation. The nature of the report changes as the years pass, first emphasizing project plans and how new faculty can participate in the decision-making. Later presentations stress the outcomes that have particular significance for new faculty.

August 1987

The first annual *Teaching/Learning Project Summary Report* is published. The format is nontraditional and designed to attract attention so it will be read by those who have become inured to packets of eight-and-one-half-by-eleven inch typed pages. A glossy, foldout brochure contains the equivalent of twenty pages of double-spaced text, broken up by photos, subcommittee time lines, calendar-style highlights for the year, and listings of persons to contact for information on specific aspects of the project. A detachable coupon offers the reader more information (for example, full subcommittee reports, prior year annual reports) than could be provided in the overview summary (see Appendices A19, A20, A21).

At the beginning of each academic year, a copy of the previous year's annual report is mailed to all college personnel. The timing is important, since the brochure informs the reader about what to look for in the year ahead. These reports also serve as the major source of information provided to outsiders who make general inquiry about the project.

Between annual reports, *Teaching/Learning Project Bulletins* provide updates. Volume 2(7) in February 1988 reviews the seven active subcommittees, reporting when each was created, who the chair is, and the status of their work.

March 1988

The first two-day retreat is held. A local hotel serves as the site and brings together 100 college personnel and guests of the college to interact over a preliminary draft of the *Statement of Faculty Excellence*. The design calls for an initial large group meeting in which McCabe delivers a charge to the group. The chair of the Faculty Excellence Subcommittee then provides background. The majority of the time is spent in small-group work sessions (see Appendix A14). Each work group is a heterogeneous mix comprised of faculty from various campuses (including members of the Faculty Excellence Subcommittee), administrators, and college guests. Reading materials have been distributed prior to the retreat, and participants have been urged to come with input from colleagues. The retreat ends in a general session with small group reports and observations from each of the guests to the college.

A second retreat is held in January 1989 to critique proposals for the various components of faculty advancement. The format and profile of participants is similar to the first retreat.

Critical Review

The number and variety of mechanisms established to provide information about and solicit information for the Teaching/Learning Project have been major factors contributing to successful implementation. Each formal vehicle worked well to an extent. The goal of keeping nearly 2,500 people on five different campuses informed is admittedly impossible to attain completely.

1. Retreats or extended sessions which were removed from daily distractions advanced the understanding of those not directly involved in day-to-day project activities. The better the understanding, the more valuable the feedback provided to evolving recommendations. These meetings also helped the project leadership step back and examine the effect their work was having on individuals who would be directly affected by the outcome.

2. The decisions made about format for the *Teaching/Learning Project Bulletin* were good ones. A single page duplicated front-to-back could provide sufficient information and could be produced easily and therefore often. The goldenrod-colored paper distinguished *Bulletins* from other unsolicited inter-office mail, allowing interested individuals to keep up with the project relatively easily.

3. Videotaping of training sessions and other critical presentations ensured that accuracy would be preserved when the content was transmitted to those who had not heard it directly.

4. Formal presentations to existing college bodies gave project personnel access to college leadership. Later in the course of the project, as support would be needed for the passage of recommendations or implementation of outcomes, there was greater chance of acceptance because of this laying of groundwork.

5. Inserting project information in existing publications made the project more a part of the fabric of the institution. McCabe's frequent mention in his own newsletter additionally underlined the importance of the work.

6. Reaching new faculty at orientation began the process of infusing the philosophy, purpose, and goals of the project in the minds of those responsible for charting the future course of the college. New employees form the only group with no unlearning to do to accept the changes the project would bring in the life of the institution. Thus this group would be most likely to implement policies and procedures as they were intended.

7. Having the source of information shift from McCabe to the project director and then to subcommittees helped institutionalize the project. McCabe's continued presence, however, communicated its ongoing importance.

Many of the negative features of our communication efforts are actually extensions of the positive aspects.

1. A number of strategies, although they had proved their worth during early years, were discontinued or underutilized later in the project. The two-day retreat, so significant in the process leading to the successful adoption of the *Statement of Faculty Excellence* and faculty advancement policies, was not used again. A retreat, providing ample time to debate complex issues, might have improved the quality of the faculty advancement procedures that were developed in 1990.

   McCabe's visits to campuses to hold small group meetings in 1987 and 1988, although time-consuming, helped him remain close to college faculty. While the project continued to unfold on schedule, the loss of his personal touch in later years was felt by faculty and perhaps contributed to a more difficult implementation of faculty advancement (see more in Chapter 6) than might have been true otherwise. In addition, extended-length sessions had helped develop in-depth understanding. There was a clear drop-off in their numbers in later stages of the project, again a probable cause of difficulties in implementation.

2. While sending *Teaching/Learning Bulletins* to all personnel effectively helped members of the institution advance together throughout the project, there was also a negative

consequence. Some groups experienced a "dulling of the senses" as they saw, repeatedly, that goldenrod communiqués did not apply to them. (This was especially the response of support staff in early years when faculty and academic administrators were clearly the project's focus.) By the time the project came to address staff, many were used to discarding the *Bulletins* unread.

We do not have a sense of whether this attempt to keep everyone equally informed has more supporters or detractors. On the one hand, we have been accused of being unnecessarily wasteful of trees; on the other hand, many support staff have expressed thanks for being included in the audience for announcements about the student feedback program for faculty, graduate courses on teaching and learning, and more. Several times readers of an issue of the *Bulletin* whom we would not have considered in the primary target group, pointed out the effect a planned recommendation would have on their jobs. They therefore had significant impact on the ultimate disposition of the recommendation. (For example: the time period selected for testing departments to distribute student feedback reports which seemed ideal from a faculty perspective, fell during a week that testing directors were already committed to processing student placement data.)

3. The frequency of publication made it difficult for some individuals to distinguish routine from critical announcements. And, ironically, while we communicated often and broadly, the project might have been served better at times if we had focused more attention on key individuals like department chairpersons, academic deans, and faculty senate presidents. Not enough communication went on at the lower levels: e.g., reports were made at college-wide consortium meetings, but not at campus faculty senates; conversations took place at President's Council but not at department or division meetings. Retelling of events often resulted in inaccurate translations. Since these translations were coming from those in authority or those held in esteem, their misinterpretations were particularly damaging to a

smooth implementation process. (More about the role of key people in Chapters 6 and 7.)

4. By 1992 we sensed that people at the college were becoming "surveyed out." What had been a very successful strategy was losing its effectiveness through overuse. Response rates that had been 50% dropped to 20%–30% by the time the Monitoring/Review Committee began to assess the impact of the new faculty advancement procedures in 1992 (see Appendix A7). Subcommittees increasingly turned to town meetings as a vehicle for interacting with colleagues. While richness in depth of exchange was gained, breadth of response was lost. Perhaps if we had been more far- sighted at the project outset, we might have better paced our surveying, foregoing use at some less important times or combining several subcommittees' needs into one instrument.

5. The degree to which the higher education community showed interest in the project was an asset when it came to broadening our perspectives on teaching and learning issues and expanding the number of strategies we would explore to reach our objectives. However, having guests frequently observing our progress added the pressure of living in a fishbowl to a climate already made stressful by the massive changes we had initiated. Whether or not the presence of outsiders limited free expression of ideas and feelings during periods of development remains a question.

6. Most communication originated in the project office, and responses for feedback or input were directed there as well. Increasing the numbers of individuals who could have been seen as project leaders or viewed as knowledgeable about teaching/learning might have increased communication foci and enhanced the accuracy of messages. The Steering Committee and the various subcommittees were not used often enough (see Appendix A3).

Discussion

The quality of the communication that is maintained between a teaching/learning project and its institutional constituency is critical to the success of any endeavor of this type.

Conscientiously attending to interactions consumes so much time that a tendency to cut corners is natural. However, in our experience, each time we neglected to adequately explain what we were doing or we failed to provide sufficient opportunity for feedback, we were forced to stop and retrace our actions. Not only does this ultimately cost more time than was originally saved, it introduces an element of distrust that can become damaging to the success of the overall effort.

Effective Institution-Wide Strategies

No single means of communication is effective with all audiences in all situations; a broad repertoire is needed. Effectiveness is situational, and depends on your audience, timing, and desired outcomes, among other factors.

1. The bulletin or newsletter. There is no substitute for putting something in writing when there is a need to create a record and to ensure that messages are precise. Lists of committee members and their phone numbers, approved recommendations, clarifications of new policies and procedures are examples of things that people would want to have for future reference. There is also an element of protection here, in that you can refer back to your files if people say, "…but, you never told us." If your institution has a newsletter to which you can have ongoing access, use it. If not, create your own.

At the same time, be careful not to put things in writing before they are ready, or without adequate prefacing. In our experience, documents with a teaching/learning association were quickly and widely circulated. In several instances drafts traveled through the institution without proper notation of their status or without adequate documentation to explain the context in which they were to be understood. Havoc followed their path.

A survey can be viewed as a variation on the bulletin or newsletter in that it creates a written record. In this case the record is of incoming communication and is an excellent reference as you build recommendations that reflect the voice of your constituency. Later in the project you may wish to document your attempts to adequately solicit input or to have a record of the stated preferences of your colleagues at a certain time. Survey data provide that evidence.

2. Meetings. To offer the opportunity for those not directly involved in project activities to hear about elements in formative stages, or to help focus issues more clearly for project personnel, face-to-face interactions are excellent. (We have illustrated the use of this strategy in Chapter 3.)

Personal communication is certainly potent and one-on-one conversations most clearly so. Interviews, however, are so labor-intensive that the payoff must truly be worth the time. Group meetings may be an acceptable compromise. If a permanent record of an exchange is important, not only should minutes be taken or a recording made, proceedings should be published for participants (see Appendix A16).

The retreat or extended-length session is an ideal way to achieve depth of understanding, air complex issues, or strive for consensus on important matters. However, because these types of meetings are expensive in professional time and money and require much effort to program, their worth must be carefully evaluated against the particular objective to be reached.

3. Reporting at scheduled meetings of college governing bodies. This mechanism is probably most effective as a way to communicate the importance rather than the substance of what you are doing. It often falls short if the objective is to get in-depth understanding or to have a meaningful exchange of ideas. College bodies meet infrequently. Their agendas are full, and their members are busy. In our experience, these factors combined to result in only the most superficial attention being paid to most items. If the members of these committees are key players in your project and you need more from them in terms of support, input or feedback, you will be better served if you approach them in other settings. In terms of what you can get that is meaningful from these visits, consider using them for the adoption phase of the changes you will recommend. (More about this in Chapter 6.)

4. Electronic communication. Electronic bulletin boards, voice mail, and videotapes have the potential to reach quickly a distant audience. These techniques (with the exception of videotapes) additionally provide opportunity for a two-way conversation to develop. The availability of appropriate technologies within the institution to support this strategy is, of course, essential.

The effectiveness of electronic communication is also limited by the familiarity or comfort level of participating personnel with the technology in question. Our own attempt to use a voice mail system as a channel for frequent communication was hampered by the failure of some individuals to regularly check for messages and the failure of others to learn to send rather than just receive them.

Deciding with Whom to Communicate

The constituency that will be affected by the outcome of the work is a logical one to address. Recommendations on support systems or workshops for faculty must be discussed with faculty. But there may be other, not so obvious, primary audiences. For example, notification that student feedback surveys are about to be distributed is important to academic administrators as well as faculty if those administrators will be expected to distribute survey packets and ensure their return for processing. An announcement to faculty that the deadline is approaching to prepare self-assessments or portfolios is also significant for the department secretary who may be asked to type them.

One way around the problem of trying to identify the not-so-obvious audience is to send general news bulletins to all campus constituencies. This way individuals can self-select to be in or out of the loop. The complaints about too little communication are more serious than those about too much. You can refine this strategy by directly mailing to the members of the principal target group and then sending a general mailing as a courtesy copy to all other personnel. This works with targeted memos carrying a broad-based list of courtesy copies, as well.

A collateral benefit of continuously informing all institutional personnel is that those less directly involved in certain phases of your project may nonetheless maintain an interest in the activities. When their turn comes, they may then better be able to philosophically place themselves in the proceedings.

Deciding How Often to Communicate

It is a mistake to limit information sharing to outcomes of significance. Frequent interchange will strengthen the end product, so you should communicate often. If you create your own newsletter, avoid a trap of making it so polished or elaborate in design that it discourages publishing except when there is something weighty to say. (For the same reason, it is probably an unwise decision to let someone else's published newsletter serve as the communications center for your project.) The detailed, written history you create through frequent communiqués may prove significant if you need to answer questions later like: Who was present when a decision was made? When did one recommendation get adopted relative to another? Who said they would take responsibility to implement a new process?

Trivializing your communications by over-production is a potential danger. "Information overload" may be a hackneyed phrase, but it is a real phenomenon. One suggestion we offer to reduce redundancy is to take a long-range view and attempt to establish in advance your key communication points. The breadth and scope of communication and strategies for disseminating or soliciting information at these junctures can be planned as well.

One-Way and Two-Way Communication

Written communication is the least effective as a two-way vehicle. Even though they demand more time and labor, town meetings, small group discussions, and interviews are more effective in eliciting a good cross-sectional response from institutional constituency and getting the affective component of information as well. People who are too busy to write their comments or who do not express themselves well in writing often respond well to an invitation to participate in an oral discussion.

These considerations may be helpful as you evaluate when to encourage or discourage dialogue.

1. Is there room to modify what you are working on? If yes, invite input.

2. Are there constraints? State them clearly at the outset.

3. Are you introducing a final product? If yes, make that clear so you do not create the expectation that feedback will be used to modify your work.

No matter how you answer the questions, a solid rule is to

progress slowly and to provide frequent opportunity for comments. Also make sure that you structure the format for input so there is a real opportunity to respond. If turnaround time is too short or no response is given, there may be an assumption that input will be ignored. As a result, response rates to later requests will decline dramatically.

Informal Communication

You will want your efforts to be talked about. While the quality of information spread informally is impossible to control, it is better to have that problem than to have no one talking about teaching and learning at your institution. Nevertheless, the quality and accuracy of circulating information is a matter that should be addressed since, as messages degrade, their content tends to become more negative rather than more positive. The degree of negativity probably is related more closely to the general climate of the institution than it is to the creative abilities of the individuals passing the messages, but it is a factor that must be considered.

How can inaccuracies be minimized? How can a rumor mill be contained? A number of strategies may lessen negative impact.

1. Continue to broadcast accurate information and invite inquiry. Publish specific names and phone numbers of individuals who are knowledgeable.

2. Respond immediately to questions and give callers more than they ask for. Turn them into resources. The people who take the time to call probably are more interested in factual information than those who never bother to verify what they hear.

3. Whatever you hear will be the tip of the iceberg; therefore, if you start to hear something several times, consider the notion widespread. Collect several misconceptions on one topic and publish clarifications in a question and answer format. Here is where your committee chairs and other project workers can be especially helpful. They not only will hear more directly from their colleagues, but they also will have more credibility than you with their colleagues and thus will be able to correct misconceptions more effectively.

While the goal of complete and totally accurate communication can never be achieved fully, you will do best by creating as large a cadre of well-informed individuals as possible. To do so requires a variety of strategies that are conscientiously and continuously employed.

INSTITUTIONALIZING CHANGE

Institutionalization is the process by which practices and attitudes are introduced into and become part of the established culture of an organization. It includes formal aspects such as the creation of policies and procedures and informal aspects such as the degree of acceptance and support given to policies and procedures. Using faculty advancement as a focal point, this chapter explores the institutionalization of change from participation to application to acceptance and the building of commitment.

Notes from the Miami-Dade Diary

January 1988

The Faculty Advancement Subcommittee is selected. The subcommittee, composed of ten faculty members and three administrators, represents all campuses and all appropriate constituencies. Six of the faculty members and two of the administrators are members of the Teaching/Learning Project Steering Committee, and all eight have served as members of the Faculty Excellence Subcommittee.

The college president charges the Faculty Advancement Subcommittee at its first meeting. The subcommittee is to make operational the work of the Faculty Excellence Subcommittee by developing processes and approaches for performance review, promotion, tenure, endowed chairs, and appropriate monetary rewards to encourage faculty excellence. The subcommittee decides that the first phase of their work will include the completion of four tasks: 1) the mental construction of an ideal faculty advancement system, including the identification of principles upon which the system rests; 2) a survey of current college policies and procedures on each campus; 3) the determination of how to alter the current system so that it will more closely resemble the ideal system; and, 4) the development of a strategy for faculty involvement in shaping a new system.

January to August 1988

The subcommittee gathers information related to an ideal system through an extensive literature search and the use of information obtained from the personal experience of subcommittee members and from the experience of colleagues. In addition, they attend a workshop given by a noted authority on evaluating faculty for promotion and tenure decisions. The subcommittee is ultimately successful in identifying several principles upon which a "good" faculty advancement system should be based.

In the meantime, the subcommittee initiates the survey of policies and procedures and their application. One part of their strategy is to contrast what is written as college policies and procedures with what faculty and administrators tell them about how the system really works. In a remarkable session with the academic deans of the four campuses, the subcommittee discovers that, even though college-wide policies and procedures governing faculty advancement exist, some practices vary so widely from campus to campus that it could easily be concluded that four separate and distinct systems are operating. Feedback from faculty throughout the college substantiates this conclusion. As they continue to gather information, the subcommittee realizes that attempting to deal with both policies and procedures is too large a task to be accomplished at one time. They decide to focus on policy and to leave procedure for a later subcommittee, an approach that is readily accepted by the college president.

Part of the subcommittee's search for a strategy for faculty involvement in shaping the new system is a consultation with a National Training Laboratories (NTL) team on the topics of improving organizational climate and communications. As a result of the NTL consultation and their continued interaction with faculty, the subcommittee determines that the following conditions must be met in order to facilitate acceptance of any proposals.

1. Faculty should be assured that their tenure and position within the college will not be threatened by changes emanating from the subcommittee's recommendations. The subcommittee believes that faculty will be more likely to participate in the Teaching/Learning Project and be more receptive to ultimate recommendations when this assurance is given.

2. There should be a transitional period in which on-board faculty who have been working toward some reward (e.g., promotion) under the old system may continue working toward the reward under the rules of the old system after new policies and procedures are operational. The subcommittee believes that a change to a new system without such a transitional period is unfair to on-board faculty.

3. Recommended changes initiated by the subcommittee should be submitted to a faculty referendum prior to official adoption by the college. The faculty should have a direct voice in decisions related to evaluation, tenure, promotion, and endowed chairs.

4. Policies adopted from the subcommittee's recommendations should be college-wide with regard to process, although substantive components may vary according to factors such as campus, department, and particular course subject matter.

5. The college should adopt some mechanism to monitor the new, college-wide policies and procedures so that there is a

uniformity of application throughout the college. The subcommittee believes that uneven application of policies and
procedures, whether from campus to campus or within a
given campus, destroys morale and undermines the entire
operation of the college.

The subcommittee presents these conditions to the college
president in a face-to-face meeting, and, after considerable discussion, he accepts them. It is further agreed that:

1. The subcommittee will make recommendations concerning
    the transitional period.

2. All faculty advancement policy proposals will be offered as
    a single, comprehensive package to be voted up or down in
    the referendum.

3. Only full-time faculty members will be eligible to vote in the
    referendum.

4. Once approved by the faculty, the referendum package will
    be presented to the college Board of Trustees for adoption.

5. Procedures to implement the new policies will be developed
    by another Teaching/Learning Project subcommittee; how-
    ever, the adoption process for the procedures, which will be
    developed by the Faculty Advancement Subcommittee and
    which will become part of the referendum package, will not
    include another referendum.

September 1988 to January 1989

As the subcommittee completes the first draft of their policy
proposals for performance review, promotion, tenure, and
endowed chairs, the college president begins small group meetings with faculty on each campus designed primarily to allow
faculty a last chance to comment on the *Statement of Faculty
Excellence*. He also uses the opportunity to alert faculty to the
work being done on faculty advancement. Meanwhile, the subcommittee produces an informational video that will be used in
other small group meetings with faculty and administrators. In
addition, they make a progress report to the Faculty Senates'
Consortium fall workshop. After meeting on all campuses with
faculty and administrators in small groups (five to fifteen persons) to explain the proposals and to solicit reactions, the sub-

committee writes a second draft of the proposals. In a meeting with President McCabe, the subcommittee agrees that the second draft of the proposals will be presented during a retreat in which selected faculty members, administrators, and guests will respond in detail to the proposals. McCabe meets with particular interest groups (administrators, full professors, new faculty, non-classroom faculty) to discuss the proposals. These meetings are intended to provide information, to solicit feedback, and to show support for the principles underlying the proposals. In preparation for the retreat, the subcommittee meets with and receives a critique of the proposals from an outside consultant.

January 1989

The retreat is held and is attended by over 100 Miami-Dade personnel and ten distinguished external consultants: Nancy Armes, Assistant to the Chancellor, Dallas County Community College District; George Baker, Professor of Higher Education, University of Texas at Austin; K. Patricia Cross, Conner Professor of Higher Education, University of California at Berkeley; Jeanne Deason, Deputy Executive Director for Programs, Florida State Board of Community Colleges; William Deegan, Professor of Higher Education, University of Miami; Russell Edgerton, President of the American Association of Higher Education; Sr. Joel Read, President, Alverno College; Richard Richardson, Director of the Center for the Study of Postsecondary Governance and Finance, Arizona State University; John Roueche, Director, Program in Community College Education, University of Texas at Austin; and James Wattenbarger, Director, Institute of Higher Education, University of Florida. The work of the retreat is intensive and productive. Participants thoroughly examine the second draft of the proposals and make major constructive criticisms, including the rejection of several specific proposals. For example, one area of particular interest is performance review, where a proposed process for "monitored improvement" for faculty whose performance had been rated unsatisfactory is perceived to lead to dismissal rather than retention.

January to April 1989

As the subcommittee analyzes input from the retreat, they begin to realize that the elements rejected deal largely with application of principles rather than with the principles themselves. Sensing that there is a broad philosophical support for the goals of the proposals, subcommittee members focus with renewed vigor on the means to achieve these ends. Within six weeks a third draft of the proposals, including a comparison of the proposed faculty advancement system with the current system, is written and distributed to faculty and administrators. Attached to this third draft is a rating survey that both compares the proposed system with the current system and asks once again for constructive criticisms to the proposals. A cover memo from the subcommittee explains that a faculty referendum on the fourth and final draft of the proposals will be held in approximately five weeks and urges undivided attention and rapid feedback so that additional good ideas may be included in the referendum package.

The subcommittee tabulates the survey results, together with information gained from special feedback sessions of the faculty senates, and uses the data to rewrite the proposals. Substantial support already exists for draft #3, but judicious refinement of that draft will increase support. Therefore, important points of concern raised in response to draft #3 are addressed in memoranda from the college president and in special Q & A *Teaching/Learning Project Bulletins* as well as in the final draft of the proposals.

The final draft is distributed to all full-time faculty, together with instructions on the referendum (when and where to vote, etc.). Special copies of the final draft are also distributed to administrators, Teaching/Learning Project Steering Committee members, members of the Faculty Senates' Consortium, and to all participants in the Faculty Senates' Consortium spring workshop. These special copies are marked to highlight important changes in wording or concept from the third to the fourth drafts. Thus, key personnel are provided with additional means to explain final changes in the proposals.

April 12 to April 13, 1989

The referendum is held, and the proposals are accepted by a 69% to 31% margin. This action sets aside important policies that had endured for over a quarter of a century and adopts new policies that reflect different philosophical assumptions.

August 1989 to March 1990

The Faculty Advancement Procedures Subcommittee is appointed. Composed of eight faculty members and three administrators, this subcommittee is to design procedures to implement the new faculty advancement policies. They survey both faculty and administrators prior to writing a first draft of the procedures.

March 1990 to June 1990

The first draft of the procedures is mailed to all faculty and administrators. The draft is discussed in detail at a special meeting of selected faculty leaders and administrators and is reviewed by faculty in general at the Combined Faculty Senates spring workshop. Basing their judgment on feedback from these meetings and other feedback obtained directly from faculty and administrators responding to the first draft, the subcommittee writes a second and final draft of the procedures. The procedures are then sent to the Teaching/Learning Project Steering Committee who reviews them for conformity with the new policies.

June 1990 to October 1990

The Steering Committee accepts the procedures as being in conformity with policy and forwards them to the faculty senates and the College Executive Committee, the final part of the official approval process. Both the senates and the Executive Committee accept the procedures which will become operational in January 1991. The implementation timetable for the new policies and procedures is presented and discussed at the Combined Faculty Senates fall workshop.

October 1990 to present

A faculty advancement design team is formed. It includes the Teaching/Learning Project Director, the Directors of the Centers for Teaching/Learning on the campuses, and a faculty member who has served on or consulted with the Faculty Excellence, Faculty Advancement, and Faculty Advancement Procedures Subcommittees. Its purpose is to design and deliver training workshops for faculty, department chairs, and administrators on all aspects of the faculty advancement process (see Appendix A8). Using this college-wide team to develop workshop content, format, and delivery should ensure consistent implementation of procedures throughout the college.

The first workshops are conducted in March 1991, and training continues to the present day. The training sessions provide an unanticipated benefit. Interaction between center directors and faculty and administrators reveals previously unrecognized problems with the procedures: unclear language, omissions, inconsistencies. These problems are transmitted to the Teaching/Learning Project Steering Committee which acts as an official interpreter of the new procedures. Clarifications are published and, of course, redirected into the training.

May 1991

The College-Wide Faculty Advancement Monitoring/Review Committee (eight faculty and three administrators) is appointed. They have two major functions: 1) to oversee the application of the faculty advancement procedures and to report inequities or inconsistencies to the President's Council and Faculty Senates' Consortium; and 2) to gather information on the effectiveness of the procedures and to make appropriate recommendations for changes concerning those procedures.

January 1992 to June 1992

The College-Wide Faculty Advancement Monitoring/Review Committee makes a preliminary report to the President's Council. It has little to report because the writing of performance reviews and actions regarding the awarding of promotions, continuing contracts, and endowed chairs have yet to be completed for the first time under the new system. In March, when these procedures are well under way, the committee surveys the faculty and administration on the implementation of the new procedures (see Appendix A7). In June the committee makes its first annual monitoring report to the President's Council. The report contains several suggestions for improvement, particularly with regard to performance portfolio preparation and the functioning of participants within the faculty advancement process (e.g., writers of performance reviews and recommendations for promotions; members of promotions, tenure, and endowed chair committees).

March 1992 to January 1993

For the first time under the new system, the committee makes recommendations for continuing contracts, promotions, and endowed chairs. These are forwarded, and decisions are announced. Many faculty members on one of the Miami-Dade campuses are upset with their campus promotions committee when it is revealed that, in comparison with other campuses, a relatively large percentage of applicants is not recommended for promotion. Many of the denied applicants appeal their cases. These appellants, whose cases normally would be heard early in the fall semester, are frustrated further by the effects of Hurricane Andrew which cause a slowdown in virtually all business and social activities throughout Dade County. Appeals decisions are not released until January 1993. In the meantime, the college has completed the second full year under the new system and is about to begin the second cycle of performance reviews and the distribution of rewards.

January 1993 to June 1993

The College-Wide Faculty Advancement Monitoring/ Review Committee, following the timetable set out in policy, surveys the faculty on the effectiveness of the procedures and puts together a set of recommendations for changes. According to policy, their recommendations are to be transmitted simultaneously to the faculty senates and the College Executive Committee, which must agree on any changes to the procedures. However, because there is general agreement that the entire faculty advancement process can be improved considerably if there are some changes in policy as well as procedure, President McCabe proposes an expanded review process. The Monitoring/Review recommendations, together with written recommendations for change from other sources within the college, become the starting point for discussions at an intensive one-day retreat held off campus. Retreat participants, who number about 100, are faculty leaders chosen by the faculty senates, key administrators, the Monitoring/Review Committee, the Teaching/Learning Center Directors, and other faculty and administrators who have served on faculty advancement subcommittees and decision-making committees. The retreat is designed to identify and obtain agreement on concepts that should be part of any changes in policies and procedures. In the week immediately following the retreat, a team of technical writers is to create the appropriate language to express the concepts, and the documents produced will then be forwarded simultaneously to the faculty senates and the College Executive Committee for debate, possible alteration, and eventual acceptance.

Critical Review

The notes from the Miami-Dade diary for this chapter have a narrow focus in the sense that they deal primarily with changes resulting from the functioning of two faculty advancement subcommittees. The Faculty Advancement Subcommittee drew up policies; the Faculty Advancement Procedures Committee wrote implementing procedures for those policies. These subcommittees, more than any others, took specific actions designed to institutionalize change brought about through the project. Thus, by focusing on the work of these subcommittees, we can illustrate many of the ideas discussed later in this chapter. Following are several positive aspects of their functioning:

1. Eight of the thirteen faculty advancement policy committee members had served previously on the Faculty Excellence Subcommittee. These people had already learned to work together as a team, and they had extensive knowledge of a concept critical to the construction of a faculty advancement system: faculty excellence. These skills and understandings would prove invaluable during the fifteen months it would take to complete their work, particularly for the pressure-packed final eleven weeks.

2. The use of consultants in conjunction with the policy committee's work was effective. It communicated a commit-

ment to strive for excellence, and it provided a source that generated useful ideas.

3. The decision to separate policies from procedures was a good one. Any package containing both policies and procedures would be too complex for a referendum.

4. Using a faculty referendum as part of the adoption process for policies was especially effective. The referendum was an excellent vehicle to aggregate support for the project in general and for the policies in particular. Also, because of the referendum results, no one could legitimately claim later that the policies were foisted upon the faculty by the administration, the kind of claim often made by dissidents at any college.

5. Including a process for the acceptance of procedures and processes for monitoring and reviewing policies and procedures was not only a necessity for getting the faculty to accept the package, but was a way of institutionalizing change (see Appendix A6). In the long run, the ultimate success or failure of the faculty advancement system and, to a great degree the project itself, depends upon the effectiveness of the monitoring and reviewing process.

6. The college president and the subcommittees established excellent working relationships as each played an active role in helping to achieve the goals of the faculty advancement program.

7. Both subcommittees provided for participation of many people in the process of drafting their proposals.

Thus, the subcommittees were highly successful in introducing change into the faculty advancement system. The process, however, was not as smooth as it could have been. Two of the rough spots were related to interactions with the college president.

First, while it is true that McCabe and the Policies Committee established an excellent working relationship, it is also true that the relationship did not always run smoothly. For example, as time passed and both the tempo and volume of the work increased, more frequent contact between the president and the committee was necessary, particularly on sensitive issues such as the degree to which the administration was willing to relinquish its considerable power in the process of faculty promotion. Remember, this committee's recommendations would be submitted for approval to a faculty referendum and not to the administration. Because of these circumstances, the interaction between the president and the committee sometimes became a form of negotiation. The problem began with lack of time and availability. There were times when the committee was ready to see McCabe, but he was unavailable. At other times, he was ready, but they weren't.

In an attempt to facilitate matters, the president and the committee chair met privately from time-to-time. The meetings focused on exchange of ideas and clarification of respective positions. Although the committee was well aware that these meetings were taking place, and the chair reported details of the meetings back to them, some members became concerned that the meetings were too "private." They indicated that they would feel better if McCabe would communicate directly with the entire committee. When he did, their expressed concern soon disappeared.

Second, there is no question that McCabe was deeply committed to and actively involved in the project. This was both a great strength and a weakness. Some faculty at Miami-Dade Community College harbored suspicions about McCabe's actions and motivations. This second-guessing of the CEO is a phenomenon that periodically occurs in virtually all bureaucratic organizations. At Miami-Dade, for example, a few skeptics asserted that McCabe's real interest in promoting the Teaching/Learning Project was to enhance his reputation as an innovative CEO. Thus McCabe, who is well aware of this kind of debunking, agreed with the Policies Committee leadership that it would be prudent to reduce considerably his visible participation in project activities during the few weeks immediately prior to the referendum. He continued to keep his distance throughout the time when the procedures committee did their work.

The discussion of a third problem area within the process requires a great deal of speculation, but is well worth considering because it includes powerful implications for the ultimate success or failure of the faculty advancement system. The Policies Committee, the majority of whom had served previously on the Faculty Excellence Subcommittee, were emotionally drained after having worked extremely hard under increasingly stressful conditions for fifteen months. It is therefore understandable that most of them had no desire to work on the next "make or break" committee, the Faculty Advancement Procedures Subcommittee. Their task, as previously mentioned, was to devise a set of procedures to implement the advancement policies adopted through the referendum. In what some might have interpreted as an act of mercy, none of the members of the Policies Committee (and, in fact, none of the members of the earlier Faculty Excellence Subcommittee) were appointed to the Procedures Committee.

Because eight of the eleven members of the Procedures Committee were faculty, and only three were administrators, it was clear that faculty would control the output of the committee, just as they had on the Faculty Excellence andPolicies Committees. This time, however, the faculty membership exercised a greater degree of cautiousness than in the past. They were concerned that none of the policies adopted through the referendum would be interpreted in such a way as to negatively impact faculty, particularly those already on board. Thus, they set out to draft procedures conscientiously designed to protect the faculty. The result of this quest was procedures that, although excellent in many respects, are too complex, overly quantified, and often redundant. For example, the performance review process includes a formal "chairperson's review" that requires the department chair to comment on whether or not the faculty member has met particular standards of excellence. This chairperson's review is to be written prior to (and in addition to) the chairperson's writing of the annual performance review. The intent of this step was twofold: 1) to ensure that faculty would be aware of any areas in which the department chair would be inclined to make negative commentary in the performance review; and 2) to allow the faculty member some time to produce evidence that would neutralize the department chair's opinion. This step has been criticized widely as unnecessary, particularly in light of the performance review policy which requires that information "that might negatively affect faculty will be documented, brought to the attention of the faculty in a timely fashion, and include supportive action when appropriate." This kind of shortcoming might easily have been overcome if the adoption for the procedures had been followed as originally intended. Unfortunately, it was not.

The process to adopt faculty advancement procedures, which had been part of the referendum package, calls for the consent of both the faculty senates (one for each campus), on the one hand, and the College Executive Committee (upper-level management), on the other. It was intended to be virtually identical to the process by which bills become acts in the U. S. Congress. Each group would examine critically and perhaps suggest additions, deletions, and/or alterations to the proposals, thus creating its own version of the procedures. Both versions would then be brought to a conference committee where differences in the two versions would be discussed and eliminated, so that only one final version would exist. This final version would be brought back to the two parties who would have their final discussions and then vote on the procedures. Those accepted by both groups would be considered formally adopted.

Instead of being adopted according to the aforementioned process, a set of procedures for the process of performance review, the awarding of tenure, promotions, and endowed chairs, and the construction of performance portfolios was accepted after minimal discussion by both the faculty senates and the College Executive Committee without additions, deletions, or alterations of any kind. It is impossible to say with absolute certainty why they didn't follow the intended process. However, after discussions with many individuals, we have concluded that the Procedures Committee lobbied the faculty senates' leadership to support their package *in toto* because: 1) "it was a good package"; 2) if the faculty were to change any of the proposals, that would invite the administration to do likewise, thus detracting from a set of proposals drafted primarily by faculty members; and 3) critical debate and alteration of the package might contribute to prolonging the process of adoption and might suggest to the administration that the faculty was not united. The senates' leadership accepted these arguments and added one of their own; by adopting the package without alteration, the senates would not only show the administration that the faculty was united, but would in effect challenge the administration to accept the package as a sign of good faith. The senates accepted the package. Finally, the administration, after learning what the senates had done, quickly accepted the package perhaps believing that alteration would be perceived as a sign of bad faith. Thus, a package that virtually everyone today agrees would have been improved considerably by careful examination, debate, and alteration, was denied improvement primarily because of political expediency.

A final bit of speculation centers around what might have happened had at least some of the members of the Policies Committee also served on the Procedures Committee. Perhaps the Procedures Committee would have had more confidence in the policies and, consequently, less of a concern with having to protect the faculty. Perhaps the Procedures Committee would have pressed to be more faithful to the intended process of adopting the procedures. Here again, one cannot be certain if these attitudes or actions would have occurred or if they would have made any difference in the outcome. We believe that adherence to the original intent of the adoption process would have slowed the process and may have caused some uncomfortable discord between faculty and administrators. However, we also believe that the procedures would have been improved, and perhaps even more importantly, that the process of ultimately negotiating a set of procedures acceptable to both faculty and administrators would have strengthened the faculty advancement system. Instead, we have struggled through a couple of years with increasing criticism of the procedures by both groups.

A fourth area in which we could have improved the process of institutionalizing change has to do with communication and understanding. The package of policies the faculty ratified was complex, sophisticated, and in many ways tremendously different from the package of policies it replaced. Even though the new policies were adopted by a landslide vote, there was no way of knowing the extent to which they were understood by the faculty or, for that matter, the administrators or anyone else at the college. The situation was analogous to what happens so often at the completion of a professional workshop: participants are asked to indicate (usually on some kind of a scale) how well they understand certain concepts or the degree to which they have acquired certain skills. The point is that they have no objective way of assessing their knowledge or skills; their ratings are purely subjective. Thus, many faculty (whether they voted for or against the package or whether they did not vote) may have thought they had a clear understanding of the policies, while actually having incomplete or inaccurate understandings. We strongly suspect that was the case. In retrospect, therefore, it would have been worthwhile to conduct workshops on the policies for faculty, administrators, and appropriate support staff personnel during the interim between the referendum and the adoption of the faculty advancement procedures. Of course, the expectation that this would have produced absolute understanding is ludicrous, but there seems to be little doubt that workshops would have reduced some of the later confusion.

Discussion

The process of institutionalizing change is perpetual and difficult. To be effective, it requires minimal participation by relatively large numbers of people within the organization and more intensive, more committed participation by a few key individuals who will ultimately make or break the process. It also requires structural mechanisms that allow for flexibility while at the same time adhering to the fundamental principles it is designed to implement. This discussion explains what we have learned about the process of institutionalizing change through our experience with faculty advancement.

Participation: Creating Reform

One of the fundamental questions to be asked when planning change is "Who will be affected by the change?" The answer to this question dictates, in a general sense, who should participate in the process. For example, in the case of faculty advancement, it is obvious that faculty should participate, as should administrators. Probably less obvious is the need for participation by the clerical staff, a group we overlooked at Miami-Dade Community College. By including them in the process, you provide recognition of their critical role in the processing of information, and you gain their input on issues such as the viability of proposed time schedules for information processing (see Appendix A10). Our failure to include them was not fatal, but the process would have been smoother with their participation in faculty advancement.

A related question is "How much should each affected group participate?" The answer to this question depends upon how much each group is legitimately affected: greater effect, greater participation; lesser effect, lesser participation. For example, of the three groups we have mentioned, the greatest legitimate effect would be on faculty, with a lesser effect on administrators and the least effect on clerical staff. Generally, we followed this principle, and it seems to have worked well. However, there was one issue that surfaced in relation to this principle, which to this day has not been completely resolved. It pertains to being "legitimately" affected. The old faculty advancement system was controlled completely by administrators; the new system would, no doubt, place substantial power in the hands of the faculty. This was unsettling to some administrators who believed in administrative control and who wanted to retain it. Thus, it was clear that administrative roles would be affected, perhaps greatly, but did that give administrators a legitimate claim to heavy participation in the process? In other words, an even more fundamental question must be answered before one can answer the question of legitimate participation: How much power *should* administrators have in the process of faculty advancement?

In fact, because of McCabe's agreement with and acceptance of faculty desires on this issue, we had an early answer to this question. What we failed to do, however, was to provide a facilitative means for administrators to buy into the new administrative posture. Workshops and other meetings specifically designed for this purpose would have been useful. Thus, we strongly suggest that you forge an answer to the power question early and immediately begin the process of acculturating appropriate personnel into any new values adopted.

The institutionalization of change requires deep commitment and substantive involvement by a few key people within the organization. Generally, reform movements require hard work and dedication; therefore, your key people should be task-oriented and loyal. Because of the nature of their collective task, they will receive criticism. It is therefore imperative that they not be thin-skinned. It is also important that they remain focused on the goals they are seeking.

There is no set number or percentage of key people required for the process to be successful. Our experience suggests that 10% of the affected personnel is more than sufficient. It is especially important, however, that some (at least 20%) of the key people be political elites—leaders who have great ability to influence others to support or reject the reforms. Common sense as well as diplomacy dictates that formal leaders (those who hold legitimate organizational office such as faculty senate president) should be involved, but do not forget to include your informal leaders, those who without the benefit of office are given deference by their colleagues because of natural or acquired qualities they possess. Participation by political elites confers legitimacy, thereby encouraging others to support reform efforts either through their own active participation or at least through passive acceptance.

Large numbers of persons need not participate in the reform process in order for reform to weave its way into the fabric of a human organization. However, more is generally better than fewer. Participation establishes and reinforces commitment: more participants, more commitment. A related principle, although seemingly obvious, is worth mentioning here. It is psychologically inconsistent to be part of a process and simultaneously to reject that process. This is one of the primary reasons why it is always better to include rather than to exclude individuals (the other is that you will get more feedback on ideas: more feedback, better product).

Two additional considerations are the overall quantity and quality of participation. There should be many opportunities for active participation in the reform process. Please note that the final version of our policies was the fourth draft of those policies, a draft that was formulated only after we sought feedback from virtually all faculty and administrators on the first three drafts, and a draft that was put to a faculty referendum for ratification. Furthermore, if the faculty had not ratified the fourth draft, we would have solicited more feedback, made appropriate changes, and submitted a fifth draft to another referendum. The point is not only to encourage active participation but to encourage it repeatedly. In addition, we should remember the previously mentioned criticism with regard to workshops immediately following the referendum. The more often you can elicit active participation, whether directly in reform or in reform-related events such as workshops, the smoother will be the process of institutionalizing change.

There is a one-word answer to the question "What should be the quality of participation?": *meaningful*. Nothing turns people off more than to work diligently to produce a recommendation that is rejected by some organizational authority. Why, they will invariably ask, did you let us continue when you knew all the time that our direction was unacceptable? Meaningful participation can be achieved only by an honest and complete charge to the committee or group of participants. They must be made aware of all constraints on their efforts and must have confidence that all legitimate (within both the letter and spirit of their charge) recommendations will be accepted. Anything less is disastrous. Manipulation will not work, nor will reform by fiat, which in our kind of political culture sometimes produces short-term efficiency but always produces long-term ineffectiveness. In short, if you are unwilling to accept meaningful participation, forget reform and concentrate on how to better accommodate the *status quo*.

Application: Administering Reform

The institutionalization of change is a three-step process that involves: 1) the creation of reform through meaningful, active participation by appropriate organizational personnel; 2) the administration of reform through the initial application of legitimately produced procedures; and 3) the building of commitment to reform through the processes of monitoring and reviewing the procedures. The section on participation has dealt with the creation of reform. This section deals with the initial application of legitimately produced procedures.

A significant question to ask when administering reform is "Should the change(s) be introduced all at once or should there be a phase-in period?" The answer depends on the number and complexity of the changes. If the number is small and the changes are relatively modest, then a one-shot, "bite the bullet" approach is useful. Conversely, if the number of changes is large or the changes are especially complex, some kind of phase-in is necessary. In our case, for example, the movement from the old to the new promotion system was particularly complex. The old system, although requiring adequacy in the performance of primary professional responsibilities and in service to the college, was primarily driven by numbers of graduate credits in-field and by graduate degrees. The new system places a premium on performance and service, requiring increasingly higher caliber performance and participation as one moves up the ranks, while at the same time placing less emphasis on credits and degrees. Certainly, it would have been unfair to require that a person only one year away from qualifying for promotion under the old system meet the new system's requirements. Thus, we included in the policies a three-year phase-in with the first year under the old system, the second year under the old or the new system, and the third year under the new system.

A word of caution is necessary here. Although there may be situations in which a phase-in is desirable, you must be careful not to extend the phase-in period too long. Often there are individuals in the organization who have an unusually great resistance to change. They will probably fight you (and everyone else) up to and sometimes beyond the time when the change is scheduled to take place. Your reforms may thus be subject to unduly harsh criticism at a particularly vulnerable time with regard to their ultimate acceptance. If the phase-in period is relatively long, these resistors may interject enough doubt in the minds of their colleagues to make the institutionalization of change considerably more difficult. Therefore, beware the overly long phase-in period.

Another important issue is the evenness of application.

When change is administered, it should be applied consistently across all units within the organization, including departments, divisions or colleges, and campuses. Uneven application presents great difficulties for the institutionalization of change. For example, our new system calls for a separate promotions committee on each of our five campuses. Although we trained all committees together in the first year in which individuals could qualify under the new system, the committees seem to have interpreted the training differently and to have approached their work in different ways. One result was that the committee on one campus had a substantially higher rate of denial than did the others. Some claimed that the committee was too hard on the candidates. Others believed that the committee acted appropriately and that the other campus committees were too lenient. Still others argued that there was really no significant difference in the overall functioning of the system on each campus because key individuals such as department chairs discouraged significantly larger percentages of potential candidates from applying on the other campuses than they did on this one. As you can easily guess, these arguments have led to considerable discontent with the system, particularly among faculty who had somehow come to expect that there would be absolute consistency in the application of procedures.

Two points are important here. The first is that when introducing change you should be especially careful to apply procedures as evenly as possible. We would have done better, for instance, by designing more detailed and extensive promotions committee workshops, perhaps requiring 100% accuracy on exit exams for individuals to become certified members of the committees. This may not have guaranteed absolute consistency in the committees' functioning, but it would have produced common understandings as a starting point for deliberations.

The second important point is that prior to administering procedures you should make a deliberate effort to educate against the expectation of absolute consistency in the application of procedures in all cases. For example, the expectation of absolute consistency in the judgments of five promotions committees is unreasonable. Conversely, the expectation of slight discrepancies in the judgments of five promotions committees is reasonable, and we should have helped faculty to understand this before our promotions committees were even formed.

Building Commitment: Monitoring and Reviewing Reform

One of the most difficult aspects of the introduction of reform is the uncertainty as to whether it will achieve its desired results. Even if it does, there is the question of whether or not the procedures employed are the most efficient for their purposes. Moreover, if the reform achieves its desired results, and if the procedures are most efficient, will both of these statements be true five or ten years from now when conditions that may have great impact on your institution change? Careful consideration of these questions leads inescapably to two conclusions: 1) monitoring and reviewing of procedures is an absolute necessity; and 2) it is wise to adopt a process for amending procedures.

The monitoring function not only facilitates the gathering of data to help determine whether your reform is working and whether your procedures are efficient; it can provide information useful in the evaluation of the performance of administrative personnel in the administration of procedures. We recommend that a committee be charged with monitoring the procedures. This committee should be composed of representatives of all classes of personnel directly affected by the procedures and should provide periodic reports to all of these constituencies.

Collected data related to goal achievement and efficiency should be reviewed periodically and used as the basis for proposing alterations to procedures. At Miami-Dade Community College we have one committee that performs both functions. They monitor continuously and review and make recommendations for changes in procedures once every three years. Collected data from our first formal review of the faculty advancement system suggest that there is strong support for the principles upon which the system is built, but that some of the procedures must be eliminated, changed, or replaced.

We adopted our process for amending procedures as part of the original reform package. This was a good idea because it demonstrated clearly that changes could be made and that we would not have to wait forever to make them, only three years.

It also spared us arguing how to change procedures at a time when we would be busy discussing what changes to make. In addition, the idea of having the retreat to brainstorm and to shape proposed changes before they went to the authoritative bodies for debate and approval is a good one. It involves many key people, including political elites, in a process that more than any other will build commitment to the faculty advancement process.

Thus, we have instituted a self-correcting method for reform in the area of faculty advancement. We recommend that you adopt a procedure for amending procedures as part of your reform, although, of course, not necessarily the specific one we have adopted. In this manner, you will achieve the desired results in institutionalizing change at your institution.

HELPING PEOPLE CHANGE

C hange is difficult, even change that has been worked for and welcomed. When individuals have help in finding their place in a new system, anxiety is lessened, mistakes in implementation are fewer, and the transition from old system to new is smoother.

Notes from the Miami-Dade Diary

September 1989

The process begins to hire a full-time director for each of the campus centers for teaching and learning. One campus responds immediately by redefining the job of a current employee. The other three campuses advertise widely. The last director is appointed in August 1990.

February 1990

The Miami-Dade Community College District Board of Trustees adopts a set of faculty advancement policies based on guidelines accepted by the faculty through a referendum in April 1989.

June 1990

A design team is formed consisting of the campus teaching/

learning center directors and Jenrette as coordinator. Napoli serves as consultant to the team. The team begins to prepare for the training that will be necessary for faculty and administrators to successfully implement the new faculty advancement procedures. Initial team meetings become marathon discussions on the philosophical constructs underlying faculty advancement and the line-by-line understanding of the proposed procedures.

October 1990

The college-wide faculty senates and the Executive Committee adopt the faculty advancement procedures. Included are performance review, performance portfolio, continuing contract, promotion, and an endowed teaching chairs program.

November 1990

Jenrette and Napoli conduct a general information session as an overview of the new faculty advancement program. The center directors are present to ask a predetermined set of questions. The meeting is held in a TV studio, and copies of the video produced are placed in the campus teaching/learning centers for later reference.

January 1991

Implementation of the new faculty advancement policies and procedures officially begins.

March 1991

One-and-a-half hour faculty advancement overview sessions are conducted on each campus. Each campus teaching/learning center director holds multiple sessions so participants can be accommodated in small groups. The largest campus, with 400 faculty and administrators, schedules twelve. The video produced in November 1990 is available for individuals who miss the sessions.

April 1991

Performance review training begins and will continue into September. The design team develops workshops for faculty and department chairpersons and administrators. The faculty sessions focus on self-assessment and the role of the individual in his/her own professional development and annual performance review. For chairpersons and administrators the sessions include practice in completing the required forms (chairperson's review, performance review narrative) but focus on the role of chair as coach and professional developer of faculty. Chairpersons engage in role playing to practice conducting a performance review interview and giving feedback to faculty on their performance. Discussion is encouraged on the conceptual differences between an evaluation system and a performance review system. Administrators are encouraged to coach chairpersons to help them effectively carry out their responsibilities under the new procedures and to evaluate their success at doing so.

May 1991

Teaching/learning centers begin offering classroom observation workshops to introduce faculty and chairpersons to the principles and practices of conducting classroom observations for developmental purposes. In the new faculty advancement program, classroom observation is an important tool for chairpersons and peer reviewers.

June 1991

Interaction between the design team and faculty/administrative participants in workshops reveals flaws in the newly adopted procedures. The Teaching/Learning Project Steering Committee becomes the body to which unclear, ambiguous, or disputed procedural matters will be taken for clarification. Results of deliberations are communicated through *Teaching/ Learning Bulletins* in a Q and A format and by teaching/learning center directors in ensuing workshops. Areas needing clarification include: whether or not chairpersons are to sit on promotions committees; what faculty who do not have regular student contact do about the student feedback requirement; how professional ethics are to be documented in a portfolio; what the real changes in performance expectations are as faculty move through the academic ranks; who "owns" the portfolio when a committee is finished reviewing it.

September 1991

A *Teaching/Learning Bulletin* alerts faculty and administrators to the faculty advancement implementation timetable and introduces a chart that organizes implementation tasks under headings by responsible parties: the candidate, department chairpersons, the administration, decision-making committees, teaching/learning centers, and the faculty senates (see Appendix A10).

October 1991

Portfolio preparation workshops begin on all campuses. Three hours in length, they help faculty learn how to prepare a narrative, how to cross reference between narrative and supporting documentation, and how to select the types of documentation that will provide evidence of having met the criteria for continuing contract, promotion, or endowed chair. Narratives and lists of documentation prepared by the design team are used in lieu of actual portfolios as examples.

February 1992

Training begins for decision makers in faculty advancement processes. Videotapes of the training are made for later viewing by those unable to attend. Continuing contract committees and departmental representatives to promotions committees are trained on their home campuses by their center directors according to the workshop design and with handouts prepared by the design team. The standing promotions committees from each campus are brought together for a single college-wide session to foster consistency in decision-making. This procedure is followed for endowed chair committees as well. College-wide training sessions last an entire day (see Appendix A8). They begin with a charge from McCabe and include a brief history of the transition to a faculty advancement program at the college, the philosophical underpinnings of that program, a step-by-step explanation of the new procedures, and practice in reviewing portfolios and making judgments based on given standards. The same sample portfolios used earlier are used for this training as well. In addition, three booklets, *Assessing the Portfolio* for promotion/continuing contract/endowed chair, recently prepared by Jenrette and Napoli, are included with other printed aids.

Department chairs and administrators who will provide input and recommendations to decision-making committees are given practice in assessing evidence and writing memos of recommendation.

February and March 1992

The first decisions on tenure and promotion under the faculty advancement procedures are made.

April 1992

Debriefing sessions begin for decision-making committees and continue thorough June. They are held approximately one week after a committee completes its tasks of reviewing all candidacies and making recommendations. Members of the faculty senates and the College-Wide Monitoring/Review Committee are invited to observe. Using a structured interview format, feedback is solicited on the new procedures, the operating practices the committees had devised where the procedures are silent, and the usefulness of various components of the portfolio (see Appendix A9). Some matters are considered potentially too sensitive to bring up in an open forum. Therefore, questions about confidentiality of deliberations, effectiveness of testimony of departmental representatives, and the quality of the training that had been provided prior to committee deliberations are asked in a survey. Committee members are encouraged to return their survey responses anonymously.

Comments made at the debriefing sessions that reveal the bases for committee members' judgments are noted. What they believe constitutes solid evidence, how they define the leadership criteria, how much data need to be presented before the "consistent performance" criterion is met, what an acceptable level of student feedback response is, how much weight the administrative recommendations are given, are all recorded. It is hoped that information from these first committees will help guide decisions of future portfolio preparers and decision-makers.

May 1992

Representatives of groups who have a key role to play in faculty advancement implementation (faculty senates, Monitoring/Review Committee, academic deans, the training design team) meet. The goals are to improve the second year of the new system by comparing notes and perceptions of the first year, to remind participants of their respective roles and responsibilities, and to surface potential problem areas.

June 1992

A *First Year Implementation Report: Faculty Advancement Promotions Process* is published and distributed widely. It details the preparation that has been made for implementation, presents composite data on the number of individuals who applied for promotion and the percentage who were successful, and makes suggestions for improvements through behavioral change and procedural modifications.

August 1992

An overview of faculty advancement is given at orientation. Because most faculty and administrators have been reached through the multiple sessions held in March and April 1991, it is decided that there is no longer a need for special sessions on the topic except for new staff.

August 1992

Second year training materials are distributed to the faculty senates, executive committee, human resources staff, academic and student deans, and the Teaching/Learning Steering Committee. Improvements have been made based on feedback from the first year. It is hoped that broad distribution will help to build a common base of information from which to answer the numerous questions about the new system (see Appendix A4).

September 1992

The second cycle of training for performance reviews and portfolio development begins. Fewer introductory sessions are offered and refreshers are introduced. After a brief review of the program, the performance review refresher concentrates on completing the self-assessment, chairperson's review, and portfolio narrative. This time examples can be used in the workshops derived from the first year's experience. Portfolio development sessions this year are specific to the purpose for which the portfolio is being prepared: tenure, promotion, or an endowed chair. This year there are real portfolios to use as examples, and the feedback from the previous year's committees tells participants what organizational pattern seemed to be easy to follow, and what types of evidence were particularly impressive. The booklet developed for decision makers, *Assessing the Portfolio,* is distributed to those who prepare portfolios the second year.

September 1992

The first faculty advancement appeals committee is trained.

October 1992

To reinforce the information being presented through workshops, McCabe, Jenrette, and the president of the faculty senates consortium write a memo. This memorandum provides information for second-year portfolio developers on effective portfolio presentation from the perspective of those who evaluated portfolios the first year (see Appendix A5). The memo suggests that faculty limit documentation to one notebook (the procedures do not officially establish limits), that they use a reference guide to their documentation, that they date their entries, and use the narrative, in part, to describe their primary professional responsibilities and components of the portfolio that might not be self-evident to the reader.

February 1993

Training begins for members of the committees who will make decisions on faculty advancement the second year. This time department representatives to promotions committees are trained in a college-wide session and their role as information-givers about the candidate or about the discipline is emphasized; that they are not designated advocates is stressed. For standing promotions committee training, sufficient agenda time is provided to reach consensus on a number of critical judgment areas to promote college-wide consistency in decision-making. The problems from the first year are pinpointed: the evaluation of student feedback; the definition of leadership and consistent performance; and the types of activities that should be acceptable toward a demonstration of service to the college.

Critical Review

As the project unfolded, it became clear that behaviors and attitudes about faculty, and administrative roles and responsibilities in faculty advancement, would have to be altered to effect substantive change. How successful we would be at making those changes would depend to a degree on the preparation, including training, we could provide to implementers. A "hold harmless" period between the time policies and procedures were

adopted and when they would take effect provided time to prepare. Even so, some aspects went more smoothly than others.

1. The four full-time campus teaching/learning center directors have been an invaluable asset in the change process.
   Three of the four have long Miami-Dade histories and two
   of the four have had considerable prior staff development
   experience. Their coming together to study the faculty
   advancement policies and procedures months before they
   would have to begin training activities helped to forge a
   team and to ensure thorough preparation.

2. Because responsibility was given to a single team who
   delivered as well as designed the training, all participants
   in faculty advancement processes were given the same
   instructions and assistance. Thus if faculty were told that
   chairpersons would be looking for reflections on strengths
   and weaknesses as they reviewed self-assessments, there
   was assurance that would be the case since the same trainers were telling chairpersons to look for reflective examples.

3. Support programs were developed and made available for
   all those who would have roles in the new processes: faculty, upper-level administrators, middle managers, decision-making committees, and appeals committees.

4. The training program was systematically planned; that is, it
   moved from a general overview of the new scheme into the
   specific program elements that were to be implemented.

5. Considerable attention was paid to involvement of all
   affected individuals, faculty and administrators alike, and
   to complete and accurate flow of information. Faculty senate representatives and Monitoring/Review Committee
   members were invited to observe all training and debriefing sessions. For example, workshops were videotaped for
   those who could not attend.

6. First year experiences were used to shape the second year
   so that problems would not be repeated. All committees
   were debriefed, and participants were surveyed. The project office reviewed findings of the Monitoring/Review
   Committee and anecdotal reports from the faculty senates,

department chairpersons, and members of the Project Steering Committee. All information was analyzed and useful ideas incorporated.

The hold harmless period was invaluable and even more necessary than we had imagined during the planning phase, yet despite the careful planning, there were still significant problems.

1. The training plan was built from an assumption that targeted populations would participate in all training and would move from one workshop to the next, smoothly and in the sequence conceived by the designers. Unfortunately, individuals participated only when they decided something was really important to them. Thus, only the most conscientious showed up for the faculty advancement overviews, and numbers increased only slightly for performance review sessions. Attendance at portfolio development workshops was close to 100% since anyone interested in tenure, promotion, or an endowed chair would have to prepare a portfolio. It is probable that attendees left somewhat confused. Our workshop design took for granted that a basic level of knowledge and understanding had been developed during the earlier two workshops, and we made no provision to accommodate those individuals for whom that was not so. In addition, we failed to hold attendees accountable for their learning. Our workshop evaluations asked participants if they felt we had met our stated workshop objectives, but we did not provide a way to assess our effectiveness in transmitting basic information.

2. The emphasis on uniform training across all campuses to assure the consistency that had been missing prior to the new faculty advancement system probably hampered effective delivery of instruction. Center directors, acting in good faith, became rigid, hesitating to deviate at all from the script, even if feedback during a workshop indicated that other approaches might be needed.

3. Direct and substantive involvement by the administration had not been an objective. It should have been. Although invited to all workshops, upper-level and middle managers

were urged to attend only those sessions that taught the mechanics of their specific role in the process. Thus, when faculty looked to them for assistance, many did not know the scope of the program, did not understand how parts were interwoven, and had not made the necessary philosophical shift to the new system. (For example, faculty advancement is predicated on a developmental model, where the administrator plays a strong coaching role, but the individual faculty member is clearly responsible for his/her own professional development. Many administrators were operating more in a punitive model.) Without the involvement of supervisors, there were too few "experts" at the college to help all those in need. Administrators who tried to help were not always successful, adding to the confusion and anxiety already inherent in making large-scale changes. Most serious, a number of administrators felt their traditional authority and position were being eroded or usurped as faculty turned elsewhere for guidance and support.

By contrast, there were a number of chairpersons and deans who had played significant roles in the Teaching/Learning Project and thus were able to help their faculty or other administrators negotiate their way through the new program. These departments were more accurate in procedural implementation and produced more successful candidates for tenure and promotion, with less anger and less frustration.

4. While participation in workshops was, and should remain, voluntary for faculty who wish to be candidates in the new system, it should have been mandatory for decision makers. The level of participant understanding was tenuous both because of the complexity of the new policies and procedures and because of the limited opportunities to practice before the actual implementation period began. When confronted with erroneous interpretations or unacceptable decisions of committee colleagues who had received no training, those who were technically correct did not always prevail. By the second year, with pressure from first year "victims," it was written in the committee appointment letter that

training would be mandatory. Since trainers are facilitators and not enforcers, however, once again professional conscience (and failing that, peer pressure) was the principal controlling force to make sure elected or appointed committee members were conscientious in this regard.

5. While successful in many ways, training activities fell short in reaching the objective of having consistency of judgments across campuses. Nowhere in policy or procedure had terms that became absolutely instrumental in decision-making been defined. For instance, interpretation of terms like "leadership," "substantive involvement in non-required activities," or "consistent demonstration of a behavior" often meant the difference between success or failure of a tenure, promotion, or endowed chair candidate. The range of professional assessments by committee members was great and produced first-year discrepancies among committees that were too extreme to be tolerated. By the second year, training strategies included consensus building on key concepts, but in many respects this came too late in the process. Portfolios are prepared in the fall. Decision makers who will assess them are trained in the following winter. Faculty need more prescription to know what types of evidence should be placed in portfolios.

6. Student feedback merits special mention. Training time must be given to data interpretation. In many portfolios, student feedback reports were the only quantified entries, and thus seemed to assume more importance in decision-making than is appropriate. Failure to come to an agreement on a college-wide cut-off score further added to the lack of consistency in decision-making.

7. We underestimated the numbers of faculty who would choose to seek rewards through one or another component of faculty advancement during the first year. Consequently, there was not enough help available on an individual level for portfolio preparation and critique, classroom observation by peers, etc. Individuals went without help or sometimes consulted with their more secure, but no more informed, peers. Advice was sometimes poor or misleading,

and accentuated the frustration inherent in a change of this magnitude.

8. While training agendas and support materials were vastly improved by the second year, many faculty who became candidates did not benefit from the improvements. Because they had participated the first year, they assumed the workshops would be the same when they were not. We should have been clearer in our communication and we should have distributed written materials to all faculty, not just to those who attended workshops.

Discussion

Those who design or conduct training sessions have a lot of power. No matter how clearly new procedures are spelled out, there are always vague or ambiguous elements in them. By necessity, the trainers will fill the gaps and resolve the ambiguities. Thus you must make sure your trainers are firmly and philosophically committed to the program as you intend it to be implemented. The performance review illustrates this point. In the performance review procedures, a chairperson's review of each faculty member was called for as a step separate from the annual performance review. The original procedures committee had meant this as a protection for faculty, forcing a chairperson to disclose any negative factors that he/she might be planning to record on the performance review itself in time for the faculty member to present evidence to the contrary. The committee was only concerned with negative observations, but failed to either design a form the chairperson could use as a checklist or clearly explain the intent. As a consequence, the center directors, reading into the procedures, designed a form that required the chairperson to elaborate on all observations, positive or negative, before writing the performance review. From the perspective of the design for a supportive, developmental system, this was an improvement. From the perspective of the busy chairperson, it created a back-breaking burden of paperwork.

What Training Can Accomplish

Training can prepare individuals by letting them practice

new behavior in a risk-free setting. It can help you determine, through practice, if an idea is poorly conceived or if problems arise because of the inexperience of the players. Quality of training alone can mean the success or failure of a new program. No matter how good a new idea is, if individuals do not know their personal responsibilities, they cannot make the program work. Make training mandatory for decision makers. Your workshops, activities, videos, and other aids are only effective if used well.

Who Should Train

When possible, trainers should have firsthand experience with what they are teaching. For example, all trainers should have prepared performance portfolios before trying to assist others in the process.

To Whom Training Should Be Offered

Training should be provided to all individuals who will play a role in new processes. Leaders should be trained first and most thoroughly. When well-versed, they should go through "train the trainer sessions" and then take over from the professional trainers. Since faculty look to their faculty senates, deans, and department chairpersons for guidance and support, individuals in these positions will make the most effective trainers in the long run. Invite observers to your workshops. They can help spread a common message and should be encouraged to do so. In our experience, those who could have been helpful but were given no role withdrew from the proceedings.

Provide for Late Joiners

Not everyone will immediately see the need to participate as you systematically introduce the components of your training program. Provide ways for late joiners to catch up with what you are doing so that they can build the necessary base of understanding to become full participants in the new program. Be prepared to have your training design evolve as your participants' knowledge grows. You will need to broaden and customize your training so that you are always working with the uninitiated, while at the same time holding refresher sessions for those who already have basic knowledge.

The Types of Training to Offer

Give individuals the opportunity to practice what they must eventually do. Role plays, case studies, decision-making simulations are all practical and helpful. Once you have begun, invite those with one year's experience to come back and help you train. They are, after all, the only true "experts." Clearly define those terms and concepts that will be pivotal in decision-making. If you have not agreed on specific definitions as part of official policy, make sure that decision-makers have the opportunity to agree to the definitions that they will be using before they are confronted with real cases.

When Training Should be Provided

When you decide it is time to train, others will not necessarily agree. Thus you may need to include in your program strategies to create a state of readiness in your audience, ways to encourage others to trust your judgment in these matters. Also, if your training program is developmental, one component building on another, you should develop strategies for involving people who skip steps. You cannot exclude them from later phases as "punishment," since even if training is not mandatory participation in the new program may be.

A final word: Training is a potent ingredient in successful implementation of change, but be wary of expecting too much from the training. We experienced the full gamut of opinion on its value. Some of our constituents undervalued the power of training in making institutional change more acceptable. These individuals frequently suggested abandoning a training session if the time to attend was inconvenient and suggested instead that we, "just read the procedures carefully. After all, we're all educated people." Others overvalued it, almost viewing training as a panacea to ensure goal attainment. There was a tendency, in this extreme, to abdicate all sense of responsibility to the trainers. "Let training fix it" and, "training should not have allowed...." Trainers should not be writing policy and procedures. With clear guidelines and definitions provided by others, however, training is a powerful tool in the process of institutionalizing change.

EVALUATING OUTCOMES

An essential component of the process of reform, whether institutional or personal, is the evaluation of outcomes. Did the changes made facilitate the attainment of goals? If so, to what extent? Are the new conditions worth the effort (time, money, energy, etc.) that was expended to achieve them? By following the guidelines presented in this chapter, you will be in an excellent position to provide your own answers to these and other questions related to the evaluation of outcomes.

Notes from the Miami-Dade Diary

March 1987

The College President, Dean of Institutional Research and several of his staff members, and the Teaching/Learning Project Director meet to discuss evaluation of the project. I R Director John Losak has already met with his staff, and they have agreed that a "before and after" assessment of conditions at the college will provide a useful basis for evaluating the impact of the project. They have further agreed that, in order to determine which areas on which to collect baseline data, a number of key personnel should be questioned with regard to changes that might occur as a result of the project. Losak explains the

115

approach to McCabe and Jenrette, and, after a discussion of expected changes, they agree to begin the process of collecting baseline data at the next Teaching/Learning Steering Committee meeting.

March 1987 to December 1987

Losak presents the approach to evaluation of the project to the Steering Committee at their March meeting. He asks them to respond in writing within one month to the question, "What do you expect to occur differently five years from now at Miami-Dade Community College as a result of the Teaching/Learning Project?" They are instructed to keep their responses brief and to write from their own individual perspectives or areas of concern or interest.

Response from the Steering Committee is anemic (only two of 25 respond), and at the April Steering Committee meeting Losak again makes a plea for input which he follows two weeks later with a memo asking for a reply within a month. Response again is low (only four more respond), and Institutional Research decides to take another approach.

At the October Steering Committee meeting Marcia Belcher, who works for Institutional Research and has been given the responsibility for directing the project's evaluation, explains the new approach. She distributes a list of goals that might be expected to be met as a result of successful project implementation, along with proposed indicators for checking on progress in meeting these goals. Steering Committee members are asked to help improve the list by providing constructive written feedback on the goals and indicators within ten days. Results are to be presented to the Steering Committee at their next meeting, in December.

Belcher presents a second draft of the goals and indicators at the December meeting. She reports that only eight persons responded to the first draft, and then leads a discussion in which she emphasizes the need for a wide variety and large number of indicators to ensure an accurate, complete picture of the project's impact. By discussion's end it is agreed that approximately one-half hour of agenda time at each Steering Committee meeting will be devoted to brainstorming on evaluation measures for project goals.

January 1988

Belcher distributes copies of the first goal (to improve the quality of teaching at Miami-Dade Community College) and indicators, and leads a discussion. Comments focus on the relationship of the indicators to those identified by the Faculty Excellence Subcommittee and on clarification of the differences among criteria for evaluation of faculty performance. As indicators are discussed, concern is repeatedly expressed about how each might only imperfectly reflect changes resulting from the project. There is agreement to focus on a limited number of meta-goals that might be accomplished in five years.

February 1988 to May 1992

Attention is shifted to recommendations of a variety of sub-committees and to their implementation. Project evaluation is placed on the back burner as energy is focused on other areas and as Institutional Research struggles to accommodate the heavier than usual demands generated by project implementation.

May 1992

Belcher presents to the Steering Committee a new plan for evaluating the project. She suggests the following approach: 1) to focus on project components that have been in place for the longest time; 2) to select readily available data, if possible, and 3) to use multiple measures and a variety of techniques, when possible. She further suggests several components that might be focused on initially, together with evaluation measures related to each. A discussion follows in which several modifications to the plan are suggested. Belcher then explains that Institutional Research does not have the resources to begin all phases at once. Therefore, she will modify the plan according to agreements obtained in the discussion and mail the modified plan to Steering Committee members with a request that they identify priorities among the plan's various components and evaluation measures. She is to report on this survey at the next Steering Committee meeting, in September.

October 1992

Hurricane Andrew dictates that the September Steering Committee meeting be postponed until October. Belcher reports on the survey of priorities at the October meeting. She reveals

that the highest priority component is evaluation of overall project impact, with the highest rated evaluation measure within
that component being student outcomes over time. It is agreed
that the college will begin to gather a variety of data on student
outcomes to study. Whenever possible, these data will be the
same as new accountability measures mandated by the state of
Florida (e.g., student grade point averages after taking sixty
credits or passing rates for A.S. students). Belcher reveals the
next highest priority components for evaluation: the teach-
ing/learning centers and new faculty. She says that she will
return to the next Steering Committee meeting with suggestions
for research strategies and with a survey that will include questions for new faculty and items related to the teaching/learn-
ing centers.

November 1992

Belcher distributes a proposal to the Steering Committee
and discusses with them ways to evaluate the teaching/learn-
ing centers and the new faculty component. She advocates
using a combination of interviewing and surveying to collect
data. These data will be combined with information already
available, including center goals, brochures, training schedules,
attendance rosters, and training evaluations. The Steering Committee suggests modifications, including the inclusion of staff
and administrators as well as faculty as respondents to questions related to the teaching/learning centers. They further recommend postponing the new faculty survey until performance
reviews and portfolio preparation are completed in February.

December 1992

Belcher presents to the Steering Committee the draft of a
survey to evaluate the new faculty component and the draft of
phone interview protocols that will be used to develop a survey to evaluate the teaching/learning centers. After discussion,
the Steering Committee approves the materials.

December 1992 to May 1993

Phone interviews to identify issues related to teaching/
learning centers are conducted, and Institutional Research
begins to develop a survey based on issues identified. Surveys on the new faculty component are distributed, and data

are collected and tabulated. In addition, Institutional Research begins to gather information on a variety of student outcomes (e.g., fall-to-winter and one-year retention data of new students, number and percent of course withdrawals and course failures, graduation rates, etc.) that can be monitored over time.

Critical Review

The weakest part of the teaching/learning process has been assessment. Teachers have done well at setting, or helping students to set, appropriate learning goals. They have also done well at creating and using appropriate teaching strategies. However, they have not been good at measuring student attainment of teaching/learning goals. Similarly, the college has succeeded at setting appropriate goals and creating strategies to achieve them, but we have not done well with regard to evaluation. Certainly, evaluation has been the weakest component of the project.

The initial idea of using a "before and after" assessment of conditions at the college as the basis for evaluating the project's impact was a good one. However, in retrospect it is clear that asking the Steering Committee to respond in writing to the question "What do you expect to occur differently five years from now at Miami-Dade Community College as a result of the Teaching/Learning Project?" was not a good idea. Perhaps the problem was in the question itself. Maybe the Steering Committee would have responded better to a proposed list of changes created by Institutional Research or to some other question. Perhaps they would have responded more completely if they had been contacted individually and urged to respond, or, even better, contacted individually and directly interviewed. Perhaps the Steering Committee was the wrong group to ask. A written survey or direct interview with personnel randomly selected from college employees might have yielded usable results. In any event, the Steering Committee's response to the initial question failed to produce information that could be used to determine which areas should be used to collect baseline data.

Shifting to a new approach when it had become obvious that the original one was not working was a good idea. Unfortunately, the Steering Committee's response to the new approach was no more favorable than their original response had been. They simply were not interested in research at a time when they were working on and debating several important early thrusts of the project. This lack of interest was eventually combined with a tremendous drain on the resources of Institutional Research (primarily in the form of helping to design and eventually processing several massive surveys related to the project) to place project evaluation at the bottom of everyone's list of work priorities.

An additional point regarding the "before and after" assessment is worth mentioning. It may have been useful at the project's outset to gather information in the form of written surveys or direct interviews from individuals representing a variety of interest groups on their attitudes toward or perceptions of practices within the college. Later, after significant components of the project had been implemented, the surveys or interviews could have been administered again so that changes could have been noted. This was not done. Of course, no one expected that the initial efforts to gather baseline data would fall victim to such a false start. Unfortunately, as a result of that false start, potentially useful data were lost forever.

Conversely, the recent report of the current status of the recommendations of subcommittees that have been created since the project's inception reveals a wealth of readily accessible data for evaluation. This report indicates that a number of highly significant recommendations intended to help the project to achieve its goals have been implemented. Among them are the creation of a Statement of Institutional Values, the *Statement of Faculty Excellence*, the Faculty Advancement Policies and Procedures, and the Endowed Chair Program (see Chapter 1 for a more complete listing and a discussion of important recommendations that have been implemented). The point is that there is hard evidence that we have accomplished much of what we set out to accomplish. However, the question of how well these accomplishments have helped us to achieve the project's goals is still largely unanswered.

The most recent attempt to focus attention on and to begin the process of evaluating the project's impact seems well timed and promising of positive results. We are now far enough into the project for many people to have become highly interested in whether or not the reforms have made significant, positive differences, and we seem to be focused on data that are capable of answering the questions being asked. Of course, it will take some time to generate sufficient data upon which to make meaningful evaluative statements. Still, we are moving in the right direction.

Discussion

Failure is sometimes a better teacher than success. And while it would be unfair to characterize our efforts at evaluating the impact of the Teaching/Learning Project as an absolute failure, we have nevertheless learned a great deal from those less than successful efforts. Several practices emerge from a consideration of our experience, and we believe these practices would be useful whether evaluating a project as massive as ours or one on a much more moderate, less ambitious scale.

The first practice is *to obtain agreement on what is to be evaluated.* This should be done at the beginning of the project, as part of the clear definition of project goals. Parties to the agreement should be the same people who formulated the goals. Obviously, a relatively broad base of participation is desirable as it will help focus attention, interest, and energy, as well as minimize confusion and argument later in the process. The participants should center their discussion upon identifying outcomes that would indicate the extent to which goals have been achieved. For example, an outcome related to the goal of improving teaching/learning might be an increase in student scores on departmental examinations in required courses. Once identified, the outcomes should be published. This published list should be reviewed periodically, so that additions, deletions, or other adjustments can be made as conditions change.

The second practice is *to determine how the outcomes are to be measured.* This should be done as soon as outcomes have been agreed upon. In practice, some consideration of how outcomes are to be measured will become part of the discussion of what is to be evaluated. The determination of how outcomes are to be measured is particularly important because it leads inevitably to a consideration of resources needed to complete the task, i.e., what human and physical resources are necessary and what they will cost.

The third practice is *to allocate sufficient resources to measure the outcomes.* This does not mean that all human, physical, and financial resources necessary to measure outcomes must be allocated immediately. It does mean that realistic budget projections for several years must be prepared, together with an understanding of where the money will come from to support these spending plans. This, of course, is bottom line stuff. If the personnel, physical resources, and money are not there when the appropriate time comes, nothing worthwhile will happen.

The fourth practice is *to provide one person with the authority and responsibility for overseeing project evaluation.* One of the most fundamental rules of organizational development is that things do not get done without a leader—not a committee or a partnership—but one person, a taskmaster. In addition to his or her stated responsibilities, this person will act as a conscience for your project by attempting to ensure that evaluation does not get lost in the shuffle, as it often does. We believe it is good practice to select and publicly announce this individual before carrying out any of the previously suggested actions in this discussion. This sends a signal that project evaluation is an integral part of an ongoing process with an importance equal to the formulation and implementation of project goals.

After having named your leader, obtained agreement on what is to be evaluated and how these outcomes are to be measured, and allocated sufficient resources to measure the outcomes, four additional practices fall naturally into place.

1. *Gather and monitor baseline data.* This process should begin as soon as possible and should be continued throughout the life of the project.

2. *Establish an archive for materials related to the project and its evaluation.* Materials might include everything from departmental course outlines or exams that have changed as a result of project activities to minutes of various committees to documented shifts in the college budget that emphasize project values. The leader could serve as archivist.

3. *Publish periodic progress reports.* These reports should be produced at regular intervals and should include considerations of all the practices mentioned thus far in this discussion. Although containing a summative dimension, these reports should be used primarily as formative tools, as a means of adjusting outcomes, measures, and resources to the changing conditions that impact your institution both from inside and outside.

4. *Publish a formal project evaluation.* This should be a comprehensive, summative evaluation of project outcomes that is published at a time that had been agreed to much earlier in the project, when the first four practices had been completed. It should include a consideration of unintended as well as intended outcomes. If yours is a long-running project, you may have to publish several formal project evaluations over an extended period of time.

We leave you with a final thought on evaluating outcomes: People are more likely to accept your claims regarding institutional reform when you have a systematic, academically defensible evaluation to back them up. This is not an area you can afford to overlook.

AFTERWORD

The Miami-Dade Community College Program in Retrospect

While Miami-Dade Community College is still implementing elements of the Teaching/Learning Project, by now we can look back and reflect on what has been accomplished and how things have worked. Our timing for beginning the project was both the best and the worst. The best because it was so apparent that American higher education, and particularly Miami-Dade Community College, needed to be the very best we could be at teaching and learning; and the worst because we were setting forth to make major institutional changes that obviously required significant commitment of resources during a period in which the state was reducing the College's income.

We simply have to get better at teaching and learning. Business and industry are, and have been, indicating that at least 80 percent of high school graduates need some postsecondary education to be employable. Further, it was clear that the stability of jobs in America was changing, and that for individuals to be employable and, therefore, able to participate effectively in the society, *all* needed to build a significant base of information skills—the ability to read, write, analyze, interpret, and communicate information. Yet, nearly three-quarters of our entering students do not possess these skills and competencies, and the problem is greatest among the poor and deprived. At the same time, higher education had done little to utilize the important research concerning adult learning, and did not have reward systems that clearly indicated a priority for teaching and learning. In addition, Miami-Dade Community College was about to lose approximately half of its founding faculty members, who began in the early '60s with a missionary zeal. They had learned a great deal, and we had to be sure that the new faculty replacing them had the same commitment to all of our constituents and that they had learned both from our veteran faculty and from research on learning. We wanted to assure that they could truly stand on the shoulders of those who went before as a basis for developing even greater competence.

The financial situation made things very difficult. At the very time that we were to proceed with the first implementation of the new promotion system and its added costs, we were faced with a $10 million reduction of a $140 million budget. I am proud of the fact that we "stuck it out," and kept our priorities. However, I am disappointed that we have had to sequence some implementation over a number of years, particularly those affecting administrative support.

We were right in getting broad participation; we were right in going step by step and taking as long as it required to gain agreement (much longer than we had planned); in having a Monitoring and Review Committee; in adopting a Statement of Faculty Excellence directly after a statement of what we valued; in holding to the idea that all of our reward systems should be based on what one does for students; and, in identifying early on that improving teaching and learning was not solely the job of faculty, but very much the job of administration as well.

Our weakest point has been in the processes that we have adopted. While we have now made the first major revision, the processes involved in the faculty advancement portion of the project are more complex than one would have hoped. Our plans were for very fundamental change in all of the processes that dealt with advancement. One might imagine, and they would be right, that this level of change brought considerable apprehension by faculty. There was concern that there could be capricious decisions by administrators or by faculty committees. This resulted in adoption of processes that were too complex, with various avenues provided to ensure fairness. The other area of concern that we are still learning about involves the decision roles in the promotion process. We have given considerable decision authority to faculty committees. This leaves some administrators wondering about their influence in the process. Yet unanswered is the degree to which faculty will make the hard decisions concerning their colleagues when they are necessary. We are making a very heavy bet that they will.

Would I lead such an undertaking again if I had the decision to make today? The answer is absolutely yes. Would I do some things differently? Some, but not too many. Making this systemic change is extremely difficult, particularly in an institution as diverse and as large as ours. However, I am convinced that we are already seeing the benefit in more faculty creativity and measurable improvement in student learning.

Robert H. McCabe, President
Miami-Dade Community College

APPENDICES

Appendix A

1. Organizing Miami-Dade Community College
   to Emphasize Faculty/Student Performance   130

2. Teaching/Learning Project Bulletin   138

3. Steering Committee Responsibilities   140

4. Promotions Process: Training Materials   141

5. Information for Portfolio Developers   142

6. Monitoring and Review of Faculty Advancement
   Procedures   144

7. Collegewide Monitoring/Review Committee
   Faculty Advancement Procedures Survey   147

8. Training for Standing Committee Members of
   Promotions Committees   149

9. Endowed Chair Debriefing Session   151

10. Responsibilities in Promotions Procedure   152

11. Teaching/Learning Values at Miami-Dade
    Community College   154

12. Teaching/Learning Project Director   158

13. President's Meeting with Senior Faculty   160

14. Retreat on Faculty Excellence   162

15. Organization of T/L Subcommittees   164

16. A Conversation About Teaching and Learning   165

17. Charge to the Support Staff
Advancement Subcommittee of the
Teaching/Learning Project   169

18. The Teaching/Learning Project is Looking for
a Few Good…   170

19. Teaching/Learning Project Subcommittee
Activities by Academic Year   172

20. 1991–92 Academic Year Highlights   173

21. Coupon   176

Appendix B

1. Principles of Learning   177

2. Faculty Excellence Subcommittee Survey   178

3. Faculty Excellence Survey
Faculty Responses   182

4. Statement of Faculty Excellence   185

5. Behavior/Documentation for Portfolio   188

Appendix C

1. Learning to Learn Subcommittee   190

2. EPS 591: Workshop in Education
Effective Teaching and Learning in
Higher Education   191

3. Authorization to Enter into a Contractual
Agreement with the University of Miami for
Graduate Instruction in the Improvement of
Teaching and Learning   194

4. Graduate Courses in Teaching and Learning   196

5. Follow-Up Survey   197

Appendix A1

ORGANIZING MIAMI-DADE COMMUNITY COLLEGE TO EMPHASIZE FACULTY/STUDENT PERFORMANCE

Robert H. McCabe, President
Miami-Dade Community College

I. THE CONCEPT

Miami-Dade Community College has an educational system that monitors and directs the progress of students through their academic programs. The system is a comprehensive structure which encompasses the total flow of the educational program. While some modifications and refinements continue to be made, the Southern Association reaccreditation self-study clearly indicated extraordinarily broad support by faculty, staff and the community for the Miami-Dade system. With that superstructure now firmly in place, attention may move to the qualitative components within.

The College has an excellent and committed faculty, and their work is the key to student success. The focus of our efforts must now be directed toward faculty development in order to strengthen teaching/learning and other functions where faculty and staff work directly with students. A strategy should be designed to ensure that all faculty and staff fully understand College program goals, and to focus efforts on attaining those goals. In addition, a system must be developed which is designed to expect good performance and to reward excellent performance. The following are important considerations in planning for advancement in teaching/learning:

A. A common element contributing to the success of community college students is the relationship with caring faculty or staff who give personal attention. Interviews with outstanding Miami-Dade faculty by researchers from the University of Texas revealed that these faculty members were interested in and concerned about their students, held high expectations for them, and consistently made themselves available to students.

Faculty increasingly hold second employment to supplement their incomes. While some can successfully combine this with a faculty career, in many cases the result is the draining of creative energies and time from their faculty roles.

B. There is a substantial body of research concerning the teaching/learning process, and much is known about successful practices; however, such knowledge is seldom utilized by faculty. Research concerning teaching/learning has become almost exclusively the province of researchers. For many reasons, including the limited academic skills of entering students, little progress is made in student development of higher-order learning competencies. As pointed out by Richard Richardson, most faculty concentrate on teaching students to learn and recall "bits" of information. However, research has produced much useful knowledge concerning teaching and learning of the higher-order competencies.

C. Institutions put little effort into developing full faculty understanding of and commitment to institutional goals as they relate to students. As a result, there is often a considerable gap between the institution's expectations and those perceived by faculty.

D. The services colleges provide can be described as a combination of personal interaction and communications. However, despite the amazing advances in communications technology, faculty have, for the most part, utilized that capability only as an adjunct tool which is supplementary to the educational program.

E. In the next five to seven years, nearly one-third of the faculty at Miami-Dade will retire. If the College is to continue to improve, the new faculty to be recruited must have the characteristics of our current successful faculty; they must also be prepared to apply knowledge gained from and through research in teaching/learning, and to fully utilize the capabilities of communications technology.

Based on the above factors, it is imperative at this time that Miami-Dade develop and implement a program which will

focus on both improvement in teaching/learning, and eleva-
tion of the status of career faculty by: utilizing assessment
techniques to recruit the most appropriate faculty; integrating faculty teaching/learning research (as proposed by Dr.
K. Patricia Cross) into the College's programs and reward
systems; relating achievement of College-valued outcomes
to evaluation, tenure and promotion; and designing the eval-
uation/promotion system to encourage full attention to faculty responsibilities.

II. THE GOAL

The goal is to institute a program in which teaching/learning is
the focal point of the College's activities and decision-making
processes. This goal will be achieved by:

A. Ensuring that all faculty and staff fully understand the College's commitments with regard to students. Outcomes that
are valued by the College will be identified, and broad commitment to achieving those outcomes will be sought.

B. Firmly establishing the centrality of student outcomes in the
total College operation by relating evaluation, promotion and
tenure decisions directly to those outcomes.

C. Incorporating what is known about successful faculty behavior and future needs of the College into the selection/reten-
tion process.

D. Assisting faculty to learn more about successful practices in
teaching/learning, and to become skilled in classroom
teaching/learning research. A graduate course in teaching/
learning will be provided by the College on-site.

E. Utilizing institutional research capabilities to provide data for
faculty instructional research and evaluation.

F. Creating a professional environment which includes recognition, reward for contributions, an attitude of respect, and
compensation appropriate for professional career teaching
faculty.

G. Providing support to faculty in their professional growth and
achievement as teachers.

H. Developing a system which will relate the success of units of the College in achieving desired student outcomes to administrative promotion and evaluation.

III. PROGRAM COMPONENTS

A. Faculty selection utilizing, as one factor, an assessment of desirable characteristics.

B. Evaluation and promotion of faculty based on educational outcomes that are valued by the College.

C. Evaluation and reward of administrators and other non-teaching professional personnel based on the educational and program outcomes valued by the College for their units of responsibility.

D. A program to strengthen faculty commitment to College goals for students, to develop their ability and skill as teaching/learning researchers, and to enhance their knowledge of research concerning teaching/learning.

IV. FACULTY TEACHING CHAIRS

The establishment of faculty chairs is a tradition in universities. Chairs provide special recognition and support for a few outstanding faculty members based on university goals. The emphasis is almost always on research and public service. Universities solicit contributions, typically of $1,000,000 or more, to endow the chairs. Holders of the chairs are additional faculty for a department, and receive payment as well as being given a budget for support from the endowment. Exceptional teaching faculty deserve similar recognition.

It would not be possible for Miami-Dade to raise endowment support for the full cost of employment for a large number of faculty. However, based on our fundraising history, it would be feasible to raise sufficient teaching chair endowment to provide enhancement for chair holders. These individuals would not be additional faculty; the College would assume responsibility for the compensation package, and the endowment would provide a supplement.

It is proposed that an endowment be raised for named teaching chairs to be utilized in recognition of outstanding teachers. Each endowment would be $75,000, and would be named for the donor. Each chair holder would receive a $5,000 salary grant annually, plus a $2,500 supplemental budget to be used at the individual's discretion for professional travel, books, materials, clerical assistance or other purposes related to work or professional development activities.

The College would undertake a multi-year endowment campaign, and would pledge Auxiliary Services revenue to make up for any shortages in endowment revenue until the endowment fund could fully support the program. The goal of the program would be a $7,500,000 endowment, producing $750,000 annually to support 100 chairs. The chairs would be established incrementally over a seven-year period. Because endowment funds would be utilized, the program would not draw from operating budget funds otherwise available for compensation; it would be in addition to the College budget.

This program would provide well-deserved recognition for outstanding teachers, and should be one more element in making a full-time teaching faculty career at Miami-Dade desirable and rewarding. It would clearly signal the emphases of the College.

V. IMPLEMENTATION

As a starting point, this document presents a major concept and the outline of a program. The program will be developed, and the ideas and concepts will be refined, adjusted and shaped, through an extensive and broadly participatory process. This is essential in order to incorporate the best thinking of the faculty and professional staffs and to ensure the wide base of support necessary for success. It is understood that this very important project will require considerable time and care both in development and implementation.

A. Establish a Staff and Program Development budget and appoint a full-time project director reporting to the President.

B. Kickoff.

    1. Retreat with College leadership (administrative and faculty) and outside experts

        a. To consider concepts

   b. To develop a process for broad participation

   c. To determine development schedule.

2. Presentation of the project and discussion of the teaching/learning emphasis at the Fall 1986 faculty senate retreat.

C. Forecast future of teaching/learning programs, including the role of communications technology.

D. Develop agreement on teaching/learning outcomes valued by Miami-Dade.

E. Develop agreement on faculty behaviors which contribute to student success.

F. Establish the staff development component in support of the project.

G. Utilization of research base for evaluation and promotion.

1. Supplied by institution

2. Developed by each faculty member

3. Sources:

   a. Student input/College-developed surveys on courses, faculty, program

   b. Retention/attendance data—College data

   c. Performance in "next" course—CLAST as related

   d. Faculty instructional research

      1) Develop graduate course concerning learning and instructional research that will be required prior to application for tenure or promotion

      2) Prepare staff development offices to assist faculty

   e. Other.

H. Proposed adjustments to promotion system.

1. Instructor/Assistant Professor rankings are one sequence. Faculty who begin as instructors, and are retained by the College, are expected to progress to Assistant Professor concurrent with the granting of tenure. The granting of tenure represents a major milestone; it follows a careful

review process and is accompanied by a significant salary adjustment.

   a. Requirements for tenure and first promotion:

      1) Completion of graduate learning/instructional research course provided on-site

      2) Demonstration of performance achievement by formal presentation of faculty research on student performance, teaching performance, and performance in other College assignments

      3) A minimum of 30 graduate credits in the teaching field (or defined equivalent for non-academic faculty).

   b. Faculty member applies for tenure after three to five years of service.

2. Promotions to Associate Professor, Associate Professor Senior, and Professor are based on faculty research demonstrating *superior* performance on College-valued outcomes.

   a. Academic preparation will no longer be a separate criterion for promotion beyond the Assistant Professor level. However, it is obviously a factor in continued professional growth which in turn relates to performance as a faculty member.

   b. There must be at least three years between promotions.

   c. Each promotion is accompanied by a significant salary increase.

   d. Each promotion to a higher rank requires demonstration of higher level performance.

   e. The two highest ranks, Associate Professor Senior and Professor, are based on distinguished performance. They are achieved by the most outstanding faculty.

I. New faculty selection procedures will include:

1. An assessment based on identified desirable character-istics.

2. A careful pre-commitment presentation on Miami-Dade program and expectations.

J. Evaluation and Reward of Administrators.

1. A performance-based system will be developed.

2. There will be faculty/employee/colleague evaluation.

3. The sum of the results for faculty/students in the area of responsibility will be an important component.

Appendix A2

TEACHING/LEARNING PROJECT BULLETIN
October, 1986

The *Teaching/Learning Project Bulletin* is a new publication prepared for Miami-Dade Community College personnel. At times
it may read almost like a diary; at times it may provide food for
thought, solicit ideas and opinions, or merely carry an announcement. It will not be published on a regular schedule, but it will
appear often.

No matter what the form, the purpose is a singular one—to
serve as an ongoing source of information about progress on
the Teaching/Learning Project.

DIRECTOR NAMED
INITIAL MEMBERS OF COMMITTEE APPOINTED

An identification process that began with a position posting in
July, 1986 has ended with the appointment of Mardee Jenrette
as Teaching/Learning Project Director. Mardee has been with
the College since 1971. Since 1977 she has been serving as
Chair of Staff and Program Development, North Campus.

At this time, during the Project's "infancy," it is especially important that you offer your comments, suggestions and opinions;
the plan for implementation should be a reflection of the real
issues confronting us. Although there will, of course, be more
formal channels and opportunities provided for you to be heard,
Mardee welcomes your contact now. She is moving to an office
on Mitchell Wolfson New World Center Campus (room 1439,
extension 73775) and, for now, can also be reached at SPD,
North (extension 71172). Feel free to call for information, with
comments, questions or concerns—or just to chat.

Your colleagues whose names appear on the following list took
part in an informal conversation about the Teaching/Learning
Project on October 9, 1986. A number of these participants (and
additional persons whose appointments we will communicate

to you as they are made) will become part of the Teaching/ Learning Project Steering Committee and can also serve as sources of information or attentive ears. Feel free to contact them as well.

We look forward to exchanging ideas and working more closely with you as the Project progresses.

Jon Alexiou	Terry Kelly	Mark Richards
Fran Aronovitz	Margaret Larkins	Suzanne Richter
Neal Benson	John Losak	Robin Roberts
Ken Blye	Jeffrey Lukenbill	Piedad Robertson
Cliff Colman	Robert McCabe	Betty Semet
Bruce Davis	John McLeod	Jeanne Stark
Henry Diaz	Tom McKitterick	Bill Stokes
Betsy Hilbert	Vince Napoli	
Mardee Jenrette	Eduardo Padron	

Appendix A3

STEERING COMMITTEE RESPONSIBILITIES

Members of the Teaching/Learning Project Steering Committee:

1. Participate in substantive discussions of key teaching/learning issues.
2. Assess needs of constituency.
3. Develop, clarify and evaluate Project goals.
4. Recommend and approve Project activities.
5. Recommend and approve sequencing and time frames of approved Project activities.
6. Review and monitor progress of the Teaching/Learning Project.
7. Evaluate progress of the Teaching/Learning Project.
8. Prepare proposals and recommendations.
9. Encourage the involvement of college personnel in all phases of the Project.
10. Act on recommendations made to the committee.
11. Communicate, as appropriate, with all sectors of the college on matters relevant to the Teaching/Learning Project.
12. Serve as advocates for the goals of the Teaching/Learning Project.
13. Lead "idea teams."
14. Serve on subcommittees.
15. Work in collaboration with the Teaching/Learning Project Director on the above matters.

Appendix A4

MIAMI-DADE COMMUNITY COLLEGE/DISTRICT TEACHING/LEARNING PROJECT

MEMORANDUM

DATE: August 11, 1992

TO: Faculty Senate Presidents
          Faculty Senates Consortium President
          Human Resources Staff
          College Executive Committee
          Academic Deans
          Student Services Deans
          Teaching/Learning Project Steering Committee

FROM: Mardee Jenrette, Director
          Teaching/Learning Project

SUBJECT: *Promotions Process: Training Materials*

Among the things we all learned through the first year of faculty advancement implementation was that consistent, accurate information is critical. As one strategy to improve on ensuring a common understanding, we have updated and made more complete a booklet we prepared last year for the training of promotions committee members. The revision is attached.

This year we will distribute it again in training sessions for members of committees, but also in workshops for faculty who will be preparing portfolios. I hope you will find it useful in your positions as you are asked to provide information on the promotions process to faculty and administrative participants.

Please feel free to request copies for others you think would find the document useful.

Attachment
cc: Teaching/Learning Center Directors

Appendix A5

MIAMI-DADE COMMUNITY COLLEGE/DISTRICT TEACHING/LEARNING PROJECT

MEMORANDUM

DATE: October 30, 1992

TO: All Faculty
             Administrators Who Supervise Faculty

FROM: Robert H. McCabe
             Bruce A. Davis
             Mardee Jenrette

SUBJECT: *Information for Portfolio Developers*

Faculty Advancement Procedure 2355, The Performance Portfolio, sets forth the required contents of the performance portfolio as it must be prepared for Continuing Contract, Promotions, and the Endowed Chair. Last year we had our first experience with the new faculty advancement program and have received information via surveys and debriefing sessions about effective portfolio presentations from the perspective of those who reviewed them for decision-making purposes.

We have distilled that information in the list below as an aid to those faculty who will be preparing portfolios this year. The same information will be communicated in Teaching/Learning Center workshops and training sessions for decision-making committees.

1. The amount of documentation that can be contained in one 3" binder proved sufficient to support a candidacy for continuing contract or promotion. Endowed Chair applicants are involved in a competitive process and may wish to present more documentation. In both cases, quality is more significant than quantity.

2. The standard Reference Guide to the Portfolio proved invaluable as committees looked for the evidence that a faculty

member met required standards of excellence. Portfolios without it were difficult to follow. The format for preparing a Reference Guide is available in the Teaching/Learning Centers.

3. Evidence proved most effective and was less easily overlooked or misunderstood when it was dated and clearly keyed to the specific standards it related to.

4. Narratives that included a description of primary professional responsibilities helped decision-makers understand the faculty member's portfolio and the documentation it contained. This is particularly important for faculty in non-traditional roles.

Appendix A6

POLICY NUMBER: II-69F
POLICY TITLE: *Monitoring and Review of*
                            Faculty Advancement
                            Procedures
LEGAL AUTHORITY: *Action by the District*
                            Board of Trustees
DATE OF BOARD ACTION: 02/27/90

   I. Collegewide Monitoring/Review Committee

In order to ensure both consistency with regard to the application of procedures for all policies designated as II-69 Faculty Advancement and flexibility with regard to the reformulation of those procedures, a Collegewide Monitoring/Review Committee will be formed.

  II. Membership

The Collegewide Monitoring/Review Committee will be composed of twelve members, nine of whom are full-time faculty members on continuing contract and three of whom are administrators. The members shall be selected through the established faculty governance process (I-80).

 III. Terms of Office

The Collegewide Monitoring/Review Committee will be a standing committee whose members serve for two years on a rotating basis in order to ensure continuity of operation.

 IV. Monitoring Functions

Two of the functions of the Collegewide Monitoring/Review Committee are to oversee the application of procedures and to report inequities or inconsistencies to the President's Council and the Faculty Senates' Consortium. With regard to these two functions, the Committee will transmit a written report of its findings and recommendations each May to the President's Council, which will review the findings and recommendations and, in turn, make appropriate recommendations to the College President.

V. Review Functions

Two additional functions of the Collegewide Monitoring/ Review Committee are (1) to gather information and to survey the faculty with regard to the effectiveness of the procedures monitored by the committee and (2) to make appropriate recommendations for change concerning those procedures—including the alteration, elimination, or addition of necessary forms, processes, and time frames. These functions constitute a formal review which will be conducted every two or three years. The review will be initiated by agreement of the Faculty Senates' Consortium and the College Executive Committee. The Committee shall transmit its written recommendations simultaneously to the College Executive Committee and the Faculty Senates at the conclusion of its study. The College Executive Committee and the Faculty Senates must agree on any changes in procedures in order for them to be adopted. Only changes in procedures that have the approval of both the College Executive Committee and the Faculty Senates will be accepted as official changes in procedures monitored by the Collegewide Monitoring/Review Committee.

VI. Goals for Implementation Schedule for Collegewide Monitoring/Review Committee.

A. The Monitoring/Review Committee will be established when the implementation of the new faculty advancement policies and procedures begins and will, as part of its monitoring function, report annually to the President's Council, beginning in January 1991.

B. The first formal review of the procedures to implement the faculty advancement policies will take place in 1992–93 according to the following timetable:

Target Date	*Committee Tasks*
April 1992	Information solicited regarding procedures.
March 1993	Written recommendations transmitted to College Executive Committee and Faculty Senates.

Agreed-upon procedures transmitted to
College President.
Procedures transmitted in writing to
Faculty and administration.

January 1994   Implementation of new procedures.

C. Subsequent review will occur every two to three years
thereafter according to the same timetable.

Appendix A7

COLLEGEWIDE MONITORING/REVIEW COMMITTEE
FACULTY ADVANCEMENT PROCEDURES SURVEY

[Excerpt]

In the spaces provided in this survey (or on additional pages), present suggestions for changes to each procedural item.
If you feel the item should stand as written, please indicate. If you feel the item should be eliminated, specify that as well. Before you begin...

1. Remember that all procedures will continue to be implemented as written unless (or until) formal changes are adopted by the Faculty Senates and College Executive Committee.

2. Read the policy on which the procedure is based to determine that your suggestions will be consistent with policy (a requirement for any change).

3. Read the procedural item as *currently* written to assure that you are aware of all details it contains.

4. Note that each procedural item is followed by page number(s) in parentheses. All references are to the procedures as they appear in "the gray book," *Faculty Advancement.*

Please return your survey by February 25, 1993 to one of the following members of the Monitoring/Review Committee:

Ken Boos	(Room 5226, North Campus)
Karen Martin	(Room 5213, Kendall Campus)
Bill Weaver	(Room 2213, Medical and Homestead Campuses)
Edwin Rivera	(Room 3403, InterAmerican Center)
Rocio Lamadriz	(Room 1641, Wolfson Campus)

I. Performance Review of Faculty, Procedure 2351. (Based on Policy II-69A on pp 7-8.)

    A. Focus of the narrative (p.9)

    G. Other aspects of the Performance Review Procedure

II. The Performance Portfolio, Procedure 2355. (Based on Policies II-69B, C, D on pp. 19-20, 25-27, 39)

    A. Length, content of narrative (p. 15-16)

    B. Required components (p. 16)

    C. Format for presentation (p. 16)

Appendix A8

TRAINING FOR STANDING COMMITTEE MEMBERS OF PROMOTIONS COMMITTEES

A G E N D A

February 14, 1992
8:30 AM – 4:30 PM
ROOM 4207
NORTH CAMPUS

8:30–9:00 am	COFFEE
9:00–9:30 am	INTRODUCTION AND CHARGE TO COMMITTEES (McCabe)
9:30–9:45 am	HISTORICAL/PHILOSOPHICAL PERSPECTIVE (Napoli)
9:45–10:15 am	ASSESSMENT OF EVIDENCE (Jenrette)

- The portfolio as a vehicle.
- Other evidence as corroboration.
- The individual must make his/her case.
- Quality and quantity (A and B standards).
- Sources within the portfolio
  - required sources;
  - recency, consistency, appropriateness;
  - primary professional responsibilities (attention to special situations; "Who's served" may not be students directly).

10:15–11:00 am	BEN JONES (Nock)

- Assessment in small group.
- Discussion in large group.

11:00–12:00 N	LIBBY BRITTON (Kah)

- Assessment in small group.
- Discussion in large group.
  (Distractors should be brought out in both discussions).

                         - endowed chair portfolios and
                             "trial balloons;"
                         - tone, style, organization pattern
                             of portfolio;
                         - comparisons ('on/off' switch for
                             standards).

12:00–12:30 pm	MAKING A RECOMMENDATION (Sharp)
12:30–1:30 pm	LUNCH BREAK
1:30–2:00 pm	FLOW OF PROCESS (AS WRITTEN) (Napoli) • Review of Procedure. • Applicable Robert's Rules.

2:00–3:30 pm	COMMITTEE LOGISTICS
	AND OPERATIONS (Center Directors
	• Brainstorm based on with Campus
	  charge, procedure Committees)
	  and rules.

3:30–4:00 pm	LARGE GROUP DISCUSSION (Lipof)
4:00–4:30 pm	EVALUATION AND ADJOURNMENT

Appendix A9

ENDOWED CHAIR DEBRIEFING SESSION
Collegewide Committee
June 16, 1992
2:00 p.m.
Wolfson Campus

1. What process did the Committee follow to complete its task?
2. What do you see as the pros and cons of the process you followed?
3. How valuable to your decision making were these parts of the portfolio…

   narrative?

   documentation?

   reference guide?
4. Did you find any common threads in those portfolios you rated as '6' (e.g., organization, expression, kinds and amount of documentation)?
5. What about those you rated lowest?
6. Were there any cases where candidates received the full range of points (1 to 6)? How do you account for that?
7. Of the 100 portfolios you saw, how many would you say were really competitive?
8. What recommendations do you have for training for…

   Endowed Chair Committees for next year?

   Endowed Chair portfolio preparers?
9. What recommendations do you have for changes in the Procedures (to be made in the third year)?
10. How do you feel about the outcome of your work on this process?

Appendix A10

RESPONSIBILITIES IN PROMOTIONS PROCEDURE

Who is responsible? → When must the task be done? ↓	Faculty Member	Department Chair/Supervisor
November	Participate in T/L Portfolio workshop (time approx.)	
December	Send letter of intent to chair of Promotions Committee; cc dept. chair by 12/15	
January	Select colleague to supervise election of department representatives to Promotions Committee before 1/15	Supervise election of department representatives to Promotions Committee before 1/15; prepare Performance Review
February	Submit portfolio to department chair 2/5	Complete Performance Review by 2/1; review portfolio and send up administrative line early in month
March	Submit portfolio to Promotions Committee by 3/1; review and respond to admin. input within 5 days of notification; make presentation to Committee if applic.	Deliver input to Promotions Committee by 3/1
April		
May	Expect notification of outcome by 5/17 (Official publication is 9/15)	

Faculty Senate	Promotions Committee	Administration
Elect standing Committee before	Elect a Chair	T/L Centers provide portfolio workshops (time approx.)
	Publish name of Chair to campus by 12/1	
	Participate in T/L training (time approx.)	T/L Centers provide Committee training (time approx.)
		Review portfolios; complete by 2/22 and return to candidate
	Notify candidate by 3/10 that all documents received; notify candidate 5 days before deliberations; make final decision during month	Deliver input to Promotion Committee by 3/1
	Send all recs. and documentation to Campus President by 4/1; communicate negative rec. to candidate within 10 days	Campus President: rec. to College President by 4/15; communicate negative recommendation to candidate within 10 days. College President: same role as Campus President if negative decision
		Notify candidate of decision by 5/17

Appendix A11

TEACHING/LEARNING VALUES AT MIAMI-DADE COMMUNITY COLLEGE

I. *Miami-Dade Community College values learning.*

To support this value, the College:

- Creates an environment conducive to teaching and learning.
- Supports life-long learning.
- Encourages the free interchange of ideas and beliefs.
- Provides the resources necessary for teaching and learning.
- Employs qualified personnel to facilitate learning.
- Provides advisement and counseling to support the needs of students.
- Expects everyone to participate actively in the learning process.
- Addresses the learning needs of the community.
- Emphasizes communication skills.

II. *Miami-Dade Community College values change to meet educational needs and to improve learning.*

To support this value, the College:

- Encourages and supports innovation and creativity.
- Responds to the changing educational needs of the community.
- Anticipates the future needs of the community.
- Supports faculty and staff development.

III. *Miami-Dade Community College values access while maintaining quality.*

To support this value, the College:

- Provides support services to assist students in meeting their educational goals.
- Offers students prescriptive learning opportunities.
- Provides occupational education which prepares the graduate to work at levels expected by the community.
- Expects students to meet defined standards.
- Provides academic programs which prepare the graduate to succeed in upper division learning.
- Provides educational opportunities for personal development.
- Structures the admissions process to encourage enrollment.
- Provides a variety of scholarships and financial aid programs.

IV. *Miami-Dade Community College values diversity in order to broaden understanding and learning.*

To support this value, the College:

- Respects individuals from a variety of cultural backgrounds.
- Provides role models.
- Offers interdisciplinary educational programs.
- Provides programs and opportunities for student growth.
- Teaches students about the cultural, economic, political, and social environments in which they live.
- Helps students to understand themselves and others.
- Sponsors academic organizations and extracurricular activities.
- Respects and responds to students' different learning styles.
- Respects and accepts different teaching styles.

V. *Miami-Dade Community College values individuals.*

To support this value, the College:

- Encourages a positive attitude toward teaching and learning.
- Stresses honesty and integrity.
- Expects all individuals to interact.
- Communicates accurately and promptly.
- Recognizes the importance of prior learning and experience.
- Develops realistic expectations for all individuals.
- Publishes explicit performance expectations for faculty, staff, and administrators.
- Publishes explicit performance expectations for students.
- Rewards achievement.

VI. *Miami-Dade Community College values a systematic approach to decision-making.*

To support this value, the College:

- Collects accurate and current data.
- Assesses the community's learning needs.
- Measures students' abilities upon entry to the institution.
- Assesses programs' effectiveness.
- Provides feedback to assist in meeting standards.
- Evaluates students' progress throughout their careers at Miami-Dade Community College.
- Encourages individuals to be aware of relevant current research.
- Surveys students' perceptions about courses, programs, and the teaching/learning environment.
- Uses the expertise of the faculty to improve the teaching/learning process.

VII. *Miami-Dade Community College values its partnership with the community.*

To support this value, the College:

- Provides accessible campus and outreach centers.
- Cooperates with other educational systems.
- Supports activities that enrich the community.
- Plans educational programs with business and industry to promote the local economic development of the community.
- Increases the community's awareness of College programs and activities.

Appendix A12

INTERNAL POSTING

P R O F E S S I O N A L   July 25, 1986

TEACHING/LEARNING PROJECT DIRECTOR

The teaching/learning project is a challenging major project to be undertaken which will place emphasis on teaching and learning. The basic concept is to ensure that teaching/learning is our central focus, and a major goal of the project will be to develop a system to tie faculty promotions and other reward systems to achievement in teaching and student learning. The project will encompass the development of a program to make a full-time faculty position at Miami-Dade a desirable and fulfilling lifetime professional career. It will also include the establishment of teaching chairs with extra awards for the most outstanding faculty, and processes for selecting new faculty who have the characteristics required to work effectively within the College's goals and expectations. We expect to begin substantial development work on this project in the fall.

TEACHING/LEARNING PROJECT DIRECTOR

When the general education study began, the College was especially fortunate to find someone with the talents of Jeff Lukenbill to lead that development. Once again, the College needs an individual of special talents and capabilities to lead the effort in this major development. Dr. Robert McCabe expects to personally give this project the highest priority, and the project director will report to him. That individual should have the following qualifications and interests:

1. Teaching experience and demonstrated teaching excellence
2. Facility with utilization of research data
3. Interest in and knowledge of developments in teaching and learning
4. Excellent interpersonal skills
5. Writing ability

6. Knowledge of Miami-Dade Community College and a commitment to the College's philosophy

7. Organizational ability

Those individuals who are interested in being considered, or who wish to nominate an individual for the position, should write to Dr. Robert McCabe immediately. Applications/nomination deadline has been established as *August 5, 1986.* Selection is anticipated during the month of August so that work can begin during the fall term.

Appendix A13

August 17, 1987

Dear_____:

As a faculty member with more than twenty years of professional commitment to Miami-Dade Community College and its
goals, you have played an important role in making the College
what it is today. I am soliciting your advice concerning our
Teaching/Learning Project. Because of your knowledge and
experience, I believe that you can provide particularly important
insights.

Accordingly, I hope they you will join me and a number of your
colleagues at a luncheon in your honor and a meeting (agenda
attached) to be held at the Radisson Mart Plaza Hotel, 711
Northwest 72 Avenue, on September 18, 1987. Lunch will be
served at 12:30 p.m.

Please RSVP to Mardee Jenrette (347-3775) by September 7,
1987. I look forward to seeing you on the 18th.

Sincerely,

Robert H. McCabe
President

wpc
Attachment

PRESIDENT'S MEETING WITH
SENIOR FACULTY

AGENDA

OPENING REMARKS: The role that senior faculty have had in shaping Miami-Dade and the potential to have significant impact on the success of the Teaching/Learning Project.

A CHALLENGE: To provide advice to the Teaching/ Learning Project Steering Committee with regard to such issues as:

- How can the new faculty member benefit from the rich experiences of the senior faculty?

- What kind of institutional support through the years has been/would have been most beneficial in aiding you to fulfill your teaching role to the best of your ability?

- What other advice would you give Miami-Dade Community College, from your vantage point, vis-a-vis its teaching/learning mission?

EXCHANGE OF IDEAS WITH PARTICIPANTS

Appendix A14

MIAMI-DADE COMMUNITY COLLEGE
TEACHING/LEARNING PROJECT RETREAT
ON FACULTY EXCELLENCE

March 4-5, 1988
Sheraton Royal Biscayne Resort
Key Biscayne, Florida

A G E N D A

March 4, 1988

Noon–1:00 p.m.   Luncheon

1:15–1:45 p.m.   Welcome (introductions, overview, retreat objectives)

1:45–4:30 p.m.   SESSION I

Report of the work of the Faculty Excellence Subcommittee

Small group discussions: Modifications to the definition of faculty excellence

4:30–5:30 p.m.   Informal interaction of participants

March 5, 1988

8:15–9:15 a.m.   Breakfast

9:30–10:15 a.m.   Small group report (panel), general discussion

10:15–noon   SESSION II

Next steps

Small group discussions: translating excellence definition into evaluation criteria, methods of evaluation, institutional rewards (issues to be considered)

Noon–1:00 p.m.   Luncheon

1:15–3:30 p.m.   SESSION II (continued)
                   Small group discussions continue
                   Report to large group
3:30–4:00 p.m.   Observations, reaction of college guests

Appendix A15

ORGANIZATION OF T/L SUBCOMMITTEES

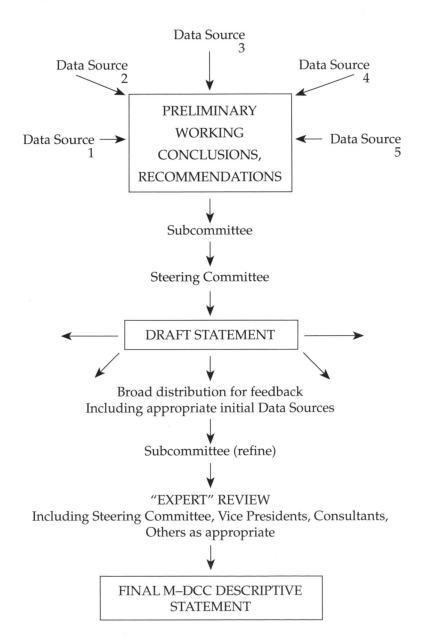

Appendix A16

October 9, 1986
9:00 a.m.–2:15 p.m…
A conversation about teaching and learning…among members of the M-DCC Teaching/Learning Project Steering Committee and invited guests

Jon Alexiou	Terry Kelly	Mark Richards
Fran Aronovitz	Margaret Larkins	Suzanne Richter
Neal Benson	John Losak	Robin Roberts
Ken Blye	Jeffrey Lukenbill	Piedad Robertson
Cliff Colman	Robert McCabe	Betty Semet
Bruce Davis	John McLeod	Jeanne Stark
Henry Diaz	Tom McKitterick	Bill Stokes
Betsy Hilbert	Vince Napoli	
Mardee Jenrette	Eduardo Padron	

Nancy Armes (Dallas Community College District)*
George Baker (University of Texas)*
K. Patricia Cross (Harvard University)*
Terry O'Banion (League for Innovation)*
John Roueche (University of Texas)*
(* Guest of the College)

Dr. McCabe provided an abbreviated overview of the concepts of the Teaching/Learning Project to establish the context in which the discussion would take place. He charged the participants, working in three task groups, to discuss the substantive elements of the project; to create a list of issues that will need to be considered prior to the formulation of a plan for implementation.

During the report-out phase of the day's activities it became clear that issues surfaced by one group were generally on the list of concerns of another. Further, upon review, the issues seemed to cluster around the broad areas of: Institutional Climate, Teaching Excellence, Leadership, and Systems. The reporting format used is a reflection of that clustering.

INSTITUTIONAL CLIMATE

"What does 'institutional commitment' mean?" is a key question. The answer will be multi-faceted and must be clearly communicated to all sectors of the College. A critical goal will be to build a collaborative model for implementation.

1. Basic to the project must be the involvement of (and control by) those who will be affected by the outcomes.

2. The institutional value base vis-a-vis teaching/learning must be clarified, clearly articulated, accepted.

3. That excellence in the classroom is a primary goal must be reflected in the day-to-day activities of all College units (e.g. Purchasing, Maintenance, Personnel, among others).

4. Communication must be established that is timely and keeps all College units up-to-date on the progress of the Teaching/Learning Project.

5. Student-centeredness must be kept as a clear focus.

TEACHING EXCELLENCE

The faculty are the Institution's single largest investment in the learning process. It will be critical, through the Project, to focus on a growth model and to set a tone of systematic, on-going support for improvement in the teaching/learning process.

1. A collaborative model for teaching/learning must be built (what happens in the classroom is in part a reflection of a number of out-of-class relationships and occurrences).

2. Faculty members must be able to get good information on their performance (in a non-threatening manner).

3. Core-competencies (derived from institutional values) for teaching excellence should be determined and

    a. included among criteria to hire new faculty,

    b. used in design of orientation strategies (for new faculty and for renewal of current faculty),

    c. made part of the definition of excellence in teaching.

4. Be clear about what outcomes (for students) are valued.

5. Diversity should be preserved, not in the "anything goes" sense, but to the degree that, while ends may need to be prescribed, means may not have to be.

6. The needs of part-time faculty must be dealt with by the Project.

7. The 'classroom research' concept must be operationally defined; who/how results are to be used must be clear; support to master necessary skills and "safely" practice must be given.

8. Establish and publish criteria and procedure for being named to a Teaching Chair.

LEADERSHIP   To a large extent, faculty motivation and participation will be influenced by the decisions made and the behaviors exhibited by those in positions of academic leadership.

1. The roles of department chair and associate dean need to be examined.

2. Academic administrators will need support and possibly training to fulfill the role of 'educational leader' (e.g. to use the tools of program evaluation, to evaluate faculty, to promote professional growth). The model, again should be growth-centered rather than punitive.

SYSTEMS   The formal systems of the College must be congruent with the stated goals of the Teaching/Learning Project if its outcomes are to be realized. The status of the teaching profession cannot be raised without superior performance being recognized and rewarded.

1. Evaluation and promotion systems need to be reviewed and

    a. must be made consistent with what the institution values in teaching and learning,

      b. must include affective attributes (with recognition that these are difficult to measure),

      c. legitimate information sources for decision-making must be identified (provision should be made for diversity),

      d. systematic evaluation of administration should become formalized.

2. (A) reward system(s) (promotion, merit) must carry specific, positive reinforcers of desired behavior.

3. Faculty load should be reviewed and perhaps redefined.

4. Policy and criteria for continuing contract should be re-examined.

5. Policy and criteria for leaves should be re-examined.

6. Redefine the functions of Institutional Research and Staff and Program Development offices to support teaching/learning priorities.

7. Identify the role that can be played in the teaching/learning process by all campus support units (including: student services, administrative services, etc.).

The lists of issues are extensive and probably not exhaustive. The items are significant and represent only a start at identifying the essential elements of this project. We do, however, now have a point of departure from which a plan can begin to take form.

Appendix A17

TEACHING/LEARNING PROJECT BULLETIN

September 1990 [Volume 5 (3)]

Two new subcommittees of the Teaching/Learning Project were created this fall term. The initial charge and membership of each are detailed here. You can expect to be contacted for input and, later, feedback as work progresses during this year. You do not have to wait to be called, however. Please do not hesitate to contact any member of either committee or me (Mardee Jenrette, X 7-3775) at any time with questions or comments.

CHARGE TO THE SUPPORT STAFF ADVANCEMENT SUBCOMMITTEE OF THE TEACHING/LEARNING PROJECT

This Subcommittee of the Teaching/Learning Project will develop a Statement of Support Staff Excellence and a set of policies and procedures that parallel, for support staff, those which were developed for faculty (and are being developed for administrators) under the umbrella heading of faculty advancement. Areas to consider will include: performance review, professional development opportunities, excellence awards, and others that may be identified by the Subcommittee as it progresses.

Additionally, the Subcommittee will recommend points at which excellence characteristics and advancement policies and procedures must differ for different staff classifications and those for which these can be the same.

To accomplish its charge, the Subcommittee will build upon the work of previous Teaching/Learning Project Subcommittees. Of most relevance will probably be: Faculty Excellence, Role of Administrators, Faculty Advancement, Advancement Procedures, and support for Faculty Subcommittees.

Appendix A18

THE TEACHING/LEARNING PROJECT IS LOOKING FOR A FEW GOOD...

We are pleased to announce that two new subcommittees will be added to the Teaching/Learning Project at the beginning of the Fall term, 1987.

CLASSROOM FEEDBACK

This subcommittee will have as its goal to make recommendations to the Steering Committee on matters including:

1. A definition of the concept.
2. The process of conducting classroom research and receiving/utilizing the feedback (e.g., Who decides what is researched? Who does the research? What support/tools are available? What happens with the resulting information? Where does this process "fit" in existing systems?).
3. A formal course in classroom research.
   A. Content
   B. Delivery mode(s)
   C. Intended audience

"LEARNING TO LEARN"

This Subcommittee will have as its goal to make recommendations to the Steering Committee on matters including:

1. A formal course in teaching/learning theory.
   A. Content
   B. Delivery mode(s)
   C. Intended audience
2. Effective student behaviors and teaching strategies to develop critical thinking skills.
3. Strategies to reinforce the College general education goal to develop the fundamental communication, critical thinking,

and creative skills in core as well as distribution and elective courses.

We will be making several appointments of faculty to work with the Steering Committee members assigned to these subcommittees. Please contact your Campus Faculty Senate President by the end of the first week of classes (*August 28*) if you would like to work with either of these projects or if you would like to participate in the Teaching/Learning Project in some other capacity (other subcommittee, campus-based activity, as examples).

If you have questions about the working of the Teaching/Learning Project, please contact Mardee Jenrette at x73775. To plaoc your name on the list for subcommitttee memberships, call:

Doug Andrews, Wolfson Senate	x73535
Neal Benson, North Senate	x71093
Ana Ciereszko, South Senate	x72589
Bill Weaver, Medical Senate	x74449

Appendix A19

Teaching/Learning Project Subcommittee Activities by Academic Year

	1987 Winter	Fall	1987/88 Winter	1988/89 Fall	Winter	1989/90 Fall	Winter	1990/91 Fall	Winter	1991/92 Fall	Winter
Steering Committee											
Values		X									
Teaching/Learning Environment			X								
Faculty Excellence				X							
Faculty Advancement (policies)				X							
New Faculty				X							
Learning to Learn				X							
Classroom Feedback				X							
Faculty Advancement Procedures								X			X
Part-Time Faculty					X		X				
Support for Faculty							X				
Role of Administrators							X		X		
Non-Classroom Faculty							X				X
Administrator Advancement										X	
Support Staff Advancement											
*Monitoring/Review											X
*Chairpersons Support X											

X = product
* = outgrowth of project

Appendix A20

1991–92 ACADEMIC YEAR HIGHLIGHTS

[Excerpt]

May 1991

- President's Council approves the addition of support staff to the Teaching Learning Project Steering Committee and the involvement of support staff presidents in the selection of representatives.
- College-wide Faculty Advancement Monitoring/Review Committee appointed and charged.
- Institutional Research analyses results of support staff excellence survey for Support Staff Subcommittee (survey was conduced in April 1991).
- Project presented: Onondaga Community College, NY.

June 1991

- *T/L Bulletin* distributed to clarify aspects of new Faculty Advancement Procedures [Vol. 5(15)].
- Visitor: Rio Hondo Community College, CA.
- Project presented: New Jersey Institute for Collegiate Teaching and Learning, NJ.
- Project presented: American Association of Higher Education Assessment Forum, CA.

July 1991

- Six additional Miami-Dade faculty complete qualifying examinations for the M-DCC/UM Doctoral program.
- Project presented: Leadership 2000, IL.

August 1991

- First payment is made to holders of the earned doctorate. (An outgrowth of the 1989 faculty advancement referendum, in which $2,000 was pledged.)

- Decision to compensate support staff at the same rate as faculty who work on Teaching/Learning task assignments.

- On North campus, renovation of faculty offices in chemistry and biology completed according to new faculty office standards.

- Analysis of two pilot administrations of the student feedback program is completed and published by Institutional Research. In: Reliability and Validity Issues: An Analysis of Miami-Dade's Pilot Student Feedback Survey (Belcher, M. Research Report 91-09R)

  Belcher concludes that the survey meets acceptable standards for reliability and validity.

- Chairpersons Support/Compensation Committee is appointed to examine the effect of faculty advancement implementation on the work of chairpersons and to make recommendations on support and compensation issues.

- Pre-Service Orientation for new faculty.

- Visitor: Dallas Community College District, TX.

September 1991

- Teaching/learning graduate courses approved by University of Miami Graduate School Curriculum Committee. New designators: EPS 539 Effective Teaching and Learning in the Community College, EPS 544 Assessing Learning in the Community College.

- Faculty receive student feedback reports from the 90-2 pilot (all full-time faculty, all classes).

- Support staff members (one representative for each employment category: secretarial/clerical, technical/paraprofessional, skilled crafts, service/maintenance) appointed to the Project Steering Committee and seated at first meeting of the year.

- Three sections of EPS 544 Assessing Learning in the Community College offered on Miami-Dade campuses.

- First administrator feedback pilot begins (North and Medical Center campus, administrators in Student Services, Academic Affairs).

- Performance Review workshops for faculty and administrators peak (begun in April).
- Visitor: Colorado Mountain College, CO.
- Project presented: Minneapolis Community College, MN.
- Project in print: *Innovation Exchange* (September 30, 1991).

October 1991

- Support Staff Subcommittee begins town meetings to finalize inclusions for the Statement of Support Staff Excellence.
- College-wide meeting of campus presidents and student services and academic affairs administrators with Teaching/Learning Center directors to review faculty advancement Implementation from the administrative perspective.
- Portfolio preparation workshops begin on campus.
- Nine senior faculty meet as a simulated Promotions Committee to review portfolio samples.
- *T/L Bulletin* 6(8) published to clarify faculty advancement procedures.
- Project in Print: Quinlan, K. "About Teaching and Learning Centers." in: *AAHE Bulletin* [Vol. 44(2)]. M-DCC one of two institutions mentioned in an article on teaching/learning centers.
- Project in print: Edgerton R., P. Hutchings, K. Quinlan. *The Teaching Portfolio: Capturing the Scholarship in Teaching.* AAHE Teaching Initiative, 1991, Washington, DC.

Appendix A21

COUPON

TO: Mardee Jenrette
        Teaching/Learning Project
        District/Wolfson Campus

FROM: _____
        Name

        _____
        Department/Extension

Please send me copies of the materials I have indicated below.

_____ Values Document

_____ Statement of Faculty Excellence

_____ Faculty Advancement Policies and Procedures

_____ Statement of Administrator Excellence

_____ Project Summary Reports from previous years

        Teaching/Learning Project Subcommittee
        Final Reports
        (Indicate which ones)

        _____

        _____

        Faculty Advancement Implementation Reports
        (Indicate which ones)

        _____

        _____

        For more information contact:
                Mardee Jenrette
                Director, Teaching/Learning Project
                Miami-Dade Community College
                300 N.E. 2nd Ave.
                Miami, Florida 33132
                (305) 237-3775

Appendix B1

MEMORANDUM   April 30, 1987

TO: T/L Project Steering Committee

FROM:Vince Napoli, Faculty Excellence Subcommittee

SUBJECT: *Principles of Learning*

The thirteen principles of learning upon which the items in the Faculty Excellence Subcommittee's survey instrument are based are as follows:

Excellent Faculty Members at M-DCC:

1. Encourage active learning in students

2. Provide adequate feedback to students

3. Accept alternatives to a linear sequence of learning by students

4. Understand how self-concept and cultural factors influence student learning

5. Encourage the use of imagery as well as rehearsal with corrective feedback to promote learning

6. Understand how the principle of transfer of learning affects student learning

7. Realize that learning is often incidental as well as intentional

8. Understand that approaches to learning may be factual, conceptual, experimental, or some combination of the three

9. Recognize that useful motivational techniques may vary from student to student

10. Understand that retention is enhanced by meaningful context as well as by practice

11. Understand that a system of assessment affects the nature of what is learned

12. Recognize that undue anxiety negatively affects learning

13. Understand that personal and societal expectations affect the level of learning

Appendix B2

FACULTY EXCELLENCE SUBCOMMITTEE SURVEY

PURPOSE

The purpose of this survey is to help carry out the primary responsibilities of the Faculty Excellence Subcommittee of the steering committee for the teaching/learning project. Our basic task is to describe those behaviors that occur throughout the institution by faculty and staff, primarily by faculty, which enhance student learning.

We began by identifying several principles known to foster student learning and development. Then, we constructed several statements that reflect each principle. Those statements constitute the items in this survey.

The items are intended to cover a wide array of functions, both inside and outside the classroom. Even though a particular item may not apply to every discipline, please let your answer indicate in general the degree of importance of the item to you. We anticipate that information received form this trial run will result in some refinement and re-thinking of the items.

DIRECTIONS

Please make a judgment regarding those activities which most enhance student learning: rank each item on a scale of one to four (low to high respectively). In addition to responding to each item, please make comments if you like.

Please circle your response for each item: "1" is the lowest rank, "5" highest.

Low   High   *Excellent faculty members at M-DCC:*

1 2 3 4 5   Encourage questions from students.

1 2 3 4 5   Review answers to test questions.

1 2 3 4 5   Allow students to take courses out of the ordinary sequence.

1 2 3 4 5   Provide initial opportunities for success.

1 2 3 4 5   Provide sample test questions and projects as examples to students.

1 2 3 4 5   Encourage students to follow a progression in course selection based on previously learned knowledge and skills.

1 2 3 4 5   Welcome student responses which clearly represent new learning but are not necessarily linked directly to material being presented.

1 2 3 4 5   Demonstrate how valid results may be obtained through both inductive and deductive reasoning.

1 2 3 4 5   Encourage students to relate personal goals to classroom learning goals.

1 2 3 4 5   Provide adequate practice opportunity to permit learning to take place.

1 2 3 4 5   Analyze questions to determine the level of learning being tested.

1 2 3 4 5   Present a reassuring and positive attitude about students' ability to learn.

1 2 3 4 5   Provide students with opportunities to set realistic goals.

1 2 3 4 5   Provide simulations with which students can explore and manipulate variables.

1 2 3 4 5   Make comments when correcting papers, not merely marking answers correct or incorrect.

1 2 3 4 5   Encourage students to explore alternatives to completion of course requirements (credit by exam, mini-term, etc.).

1 2 3 4 5   Criticize students' performance rather than the students themselves.

1 2 3 4 5   Require students to provide examples of concepts.

1 2 3 4 5   Go over tests as a means of teaching as well as providing feedback.

1 2 3 4 5   Ask questions that encourage independent thinking.

1 2 3 4 5   Show how principles can be used to remember facts and facts can be used to remember principles.

1 2 3 4 5   Use reinforcement that is appropriate to the learning situation.

1 2 3 4 5   Use examples to show students how to apply what they have learned to situations outside the classroom.

1 2 3 4 5   Use several methods to assess student learning.

1 2 3 4 5   Encourage students to approach them, thereby reducing student anxieties.

1 2 3 4 5   Maintain high performance goals for themselves.

1 2 3 4 5   Encourage students to do independent research in the library.

1 2 3 4 5   Return tests, reports, papers, etc. to students in a timely manner.

1 2 3 4 5   Grant credit for topics of interest to students, provided they are within the framework of the course.

1 2 3 4 5   Promote and encourage participation in cultural activities.

1 2 3 4 5   Ask students to go through the steps of an experiment mentally before actually performing the experiment.

1 2 3 4 5   Point out relationships between previous concepts and material currently being presented.

1 2 3 4 5   Allow students to write on topics that deviate from the original assignment (after discussion with the instructor).

1 2 3 4 5   Emphasize ideas, principles, and theories as well as facts.

1 2 3 4 5   Select strategies that are appropriate to the level of student learning/motivation.

1 2 3 4 5   Restate major concepts using different modalities of expression.

1 2 3 4 5 Review test items with students to clarify what has been learned.

1 2 3 4 5 Use appropriate techniques to reduce anxiety in testing situations.

1 2 3 4 5 Encourage students to set high performance goals for themselves.

1 2 3 4 5 Encourage students to relate subject matter to personal experiences.

1 2 3 4 5 Provide constructive advice to students with regard to their proposed course selection.

1 2 3 4 5 Allow students to select articles from a referenced list of topics.

1 2 3 4 5 Allow students to write about or to present material related to their own culture.

1 2 3 4 5 Explain correct responses by using examples.

1 2 3 4 5 Build a framework for students to progress from observations to conclusions.

1 2 3 4 5 Invite guest speakers and demonstrators.

1 2 3 4 5 Encourage students to learn through outside activities such as field trips.

1 2 3 4 5 Provide exercises and assignments which relate to specific careers.

1 2 3 4 5 Provide assessment devices that measure what was taught in the classroom.

1 2 3 4 5 Encourage students to learn and to use relaxation techniques to deal with anxiety.

1 2 3 4 5 Encourage and promote discussion of how society views and values the subject-matter being taught.

1 2 3 4 5 Re-evaluate student learning as a result of instructor feedback.

1 2 3 4 5 Explain evaluation system to students.

Appendix B3

FACULTY EXCELLENCE SURVEY
Faculty Responses
(Response Rate 40%)

PURPOSE

The purpose of this survey is to help carry out the primary responsibilities of the Faculty Excellence Subcommittee of the Steering Committee for the Teaching/Learning project. Our basic task is to describe those faculty behaviors/attitudes which enhance student learning throughout the institution. The 28 items have been selected after careful review of the literature and feedback obtained from Miami-Dade Community College faculty. Although we believe that all 28 behaviors/attitudes enhance student learning, we are asking that you rate each item, high to low, based on your views.

The items are intended to cover a wide array of functions, both inside and outside the classroom. Even though a particular item may not apply to every discipline, please let your answer indicate in general the degree of importance of the item to you.

DIRECTIONS

Please make a judgment regarding those activities which most enhance student learning: rank each item on a scale of one to four (low to high respectively). In addition to responding to each item, please make comments in the space provided.

Please mark on the answer sheet: "1" is the lowest rating, "4" is the highest.

Excellent faculty members at M-DCC, whether classroom teachers, librarians, counselors, or serving in any other faculty capacity:

N = 325

Low 1	2	3	High 4	
	2%	15%	83%	1. Are enthusiastic about their work.
	1%	11%	88%	2. Present ideas clearly.
	4%	22%	74%	3. Do their work in a well prepared manner.
		11%	89%	4. Are knowledgeable about their work.
	4%	28%	68%	5. Are responsive to student needs.
1%	8%	35%	57%	6. Set challenging performance goals for students.
1%	9%	31%	59%	7. Set challenging performance goals for themselves.
	6%	31%	64%	8. Give corrective feedback promptly to students.
	1%	16%	83%	9. Are fair in their evaluations of student progress.
	4%	26%	71%	10. Listen attentively to what students say.
2%	15%	35%	48%	11. See students as individuals operating in a broader perspective beyond the classroom.
3%	11%	29%	57%	12. Are committed to education as a profession.
	5%	31%	65%	13. Use teaching techniques that stimulate intellectual curiosity.
1%	14%	34%	51%	14. Respect diverse talents.
	5%	25%	70%	15. Project a positive attitude about their students' ability to learn.
	1%	15%	84%	16 Treat students with respect.

2% 6% 26% 66%   17. Display behavior consistent with professional standards.

   6% 33% 60%   18. Are available to students.

2% 13% 31% 54%   19. Provide scholarly perspectives that include a respect for diverse views.

4% 8% 23% 65%   20. Provide a written statement of course requirements and evaluation procedures at the beginning of the semester.

   8% 34% 58%   21. Use teaching techniques that develop independent thinking.

1% 6% 30% 63%   22. Integrate current subject matter knowledge into their work.

1% 8% 35% 57%   23. Encourage students to be analytical listeners.

3% 16% 39% 43%   24. Provide students with alternative ways of learning.

3% 13% 36% 48%   25. Display a genuine sense of humor conducive to a positive teacher/student relationship.

4% 8% 35% 53%   26. Provide clear and substantial evidence that students have learned.

1% 8% 33% 58%   27. Give consideration to feedback from students and others.

2% 8% 30% 61%   28. Do their work in a well organized manner.

Appendix B4

STATEMENT OF FACULTY EXCELLENCE [Excerpt]

MOTIVATION

Excellent faculty at Miami-Dade Community College are dedicated to their profession in higher education and to the community college philosophy as defined at Miami-Dade. Their
greatest concern is for student learning; thus, they themselves
are highly motivated to achieve excellence and to strive to motivate students to reach their educational and personal goals.

Excellent faculty at Miami-Dade *are enthusiastic about their work.*
Faculty, administrators, and students all regard enthusiasm as a
primary motivational factor. Faculty manifest this enthusiasm in a
variety of ways. They communicate their deep interest in their discipline fields and the satisfaction they themselves have gained
through increasing their knowledge. Faculty demonstrate their
enthusiasm in their professional areas by willingly working in a
personal way with students or prospective students to help them
achieve their goals. Faculty share with students and colleagues
the rewards of their involvement in their professional organizations and associations. They build in students a sense of accom-
plishment when they demonstrate their learning and they instill in
them both the desire and self-confidence needed to increase their
learning. In short, they communicate the values and satisfactions
to be gained in the teaching and learning activity.

Excellent faculty at Miami-Dade *set challenging individual and
collective performance goals for themselves.* These goals
address not only learning activities and other specific academic
responsibilities, but also the many other areas of professional
involvement. They continually strive to increase their own knowledge and to perfect their job-related skills, practices, and procedures. In so doing, they serve as positive role models for both
students and colleagues.

Excellent faculty at Miami-Dade also *set challenging performance goals for students.* They communicate to students that
progress is not made without a cost; it must be paid for in time

and effort. Thus, they encourage students to overcome their limitations and to reach beyond their current achievements in an attempt to fulfill all of their potential.

Excellent faculty at Miami-Dade *are committed to education as a profession.* They value their work highly because of the intrinsic satisfaction they receive from knowing they have helped students to learn and to succeed in their lives. Regardless of circumstances, commitment to their students does not waver.

Excellent faculty, who are committed to the mission and values of Miami-Dade, *project a positive attitude about students' ability to learn.* Outstanding faculty have a strong commitment to the open door policy; they believe that students with diverse needs can learn and so they challenge them accordingly. This belief is, no doubt, a motivating factor for both students and faculty.

Excellent faculty at Miami-Dade *display behavior consistent with professional ethics.* They are aware that a failure to commit to professional standards weakens the profession. They guard against behavior that may detract from the teaching/learning process. Thus, these faculty maintain the most professional and ethical relationships with students and colleagues.

Finally, excellent faculty *are concerned with the many aspects of students as individuals, not just in their roles as learners.* Accordingly, they provide counsel and assistance whenever appropriate.

KNOWLEDGE BASE

Excellent faculty at Miami-Dade Community College have the intellectual skills and knowledge requisite for superlative performance. They have a thorough understanding not only of their own work areas and disciplines, but also of how students learn and develop. This knowledge base is essential in their work within the context of Miami-Dade's open admissions policy.

Fundamental to excellence, according to faculty, administrators, and students, is that faculty members at Miami-Dade *are knowledgeable about their work areas and disciplines.* This knowledge includes not only the content of the disciplines, but also their roles in their departments and their campus in support of the overall teaching and learning process. These faculty also share their knowledge with one another in a collegial effort to achieve excellence. There is no substitute for faculty members' having in-depth knowledge of their fields and disciplines in order to facilitate the transfer of knowledge to students. Without substantial knowledge in their fields, faculty are ill-prepared to foster student learning, even if their motivational techniques and interpersonal skills are sound.

Excellent faculty at Miami-Dade *are knowledgeable about how students learn.* They understand established principles of learning which serve as a foundation for their work with students as they advise, teach and provide learning support. This knowledge encompasses the many differences in students which, in part, stem from the great cultural diversity found on the Miami-Dade campuses.

Excellent faculty at Miami-Dade *integrate current subject matter into their work.* Students should have information and the results of research and study which reflect the latest work in the field. Excellent faculty consistently update their own knowledge, professional skills, and resources to make their instruction meaningful, timely, and refreshing to their students.

Excellent faculty at Miami-Dade also *provide perspectives that include a respect for diverse views.* They provide a variety of theories and interpretations that represent the best thinking in their fields. Moreover, they demonstrate to their students an openness and willingness to communicate and share differing views. These excellent faculty are particularly sensitive to Miami-Dade's diverse student body, which represents a wide variety of cultures and academic traditions.

Excellent faculty at Miami-Dade *do their work in a well-prepared and well-organized manner.* Faculty have clear learning goals and well planned activities enabling students to master content material and to process and apply information. Faculty proceed logically and use time effectively so that students learn as much as possible. Faculty provide assistance to students in a clear manner so that they know and can use the College's educational systems effectively.

Appendix B5

BEHAVIOR/DOCUMENTATION FOR PORTFOLIO
[Excerpt]

Concern with students as individuals

- Distributes to students a statement of personal teaching/ learning philosophy (example).
- Comments on students' concerns gathered through classroom assessment techniques (chair/peer obs., unsolicited letters of appreciation from students).
- Provides written feedback on papers and tests (examples).
- Learns and uses names of students (chair/peer obs.).
- Offers students choices, as appropriate, to meet course objectives (contract grading).
- Participates in extracurricular activities with students (memo, letters).
- Serves as mentor/facilitator for students (memos, record of visits).
- Invites students for individual conferences (appointment log).

Treat individuals with respect (* Peers, chair, students)

- Uses sound feedback techniques (student feedback, obs. by peer/chair).
- Develops and distributes guidelines for students to give constructive feedback to one another (example).

Respect talents

- Increases knowledge of learning styles (evidence of readings, attendance at courses/workshops).
- Addresses differences in learning styles through coursework (peer/chair obs., examples of assignments, activities).
- Assesses learning styles of students (examples of instruments).

- Uses a variety of instructional strategies to address a variety of learning styles (chair/peer obs., lesson plans).

Work collaboratively (* Peers, chairs)

- Contributes as a committee member (testimony from committee chair).
- Participates in team teaching activities (examples, peer testimony).
- Participates in publishing, authoring activities (examples).
- Gives guest presentations (examples).
- Openly demonstrates support for colleagues (peer/chair direct obs.).

Available to students

- Sponsors a student organization (memos, minutes).
- Establishes and meets with student "feedback" groups (student feedback, peer testimony, student handouts).
- Is early for class, stays during breaks, and allows time for student contact after class (student feedback, log, handout).
- Attends extracurricular functions in which students participate (peer testimony, chair observations).
- Maintains office hours that meet student needs (weekly schedule, student feedback, peer testimony).

Appendix C1

M E M O R A N D U M   February 26, 1988

TO: M-DCC Faculty

FROM: Learning to Learn Subcommittee
        Teaching/Learning Project

Many faculty begin at M-DCC unaware of the characteristics of our student population or perhaps with little or no exposure to alternative teaching strategies. We are designing a course to help new faculty who will come to M-DCC. We need your help. Please take a few moments to share your thoughts on the following question:

> Given your level of experience with teaching and learning, what content do you recommend for a faculty course designed to enhance student learning? Discuss (1) general knowledge and skills, (2) concepts specific to M-DCC, and (3) concepts specific to your discipline or area.

Please return your answers to Robin Roberts, English Department, South Campus. If you would prefer to be interviewed or wish to speak with any members of the subcommittee, contact one of the following:

Joann Brown, Medical	74421
Robin Roberts, South	72511
Harry Hoffman, Wolfson	73151
Piedad Robertson, District	72020
Jim Lamar, North	71290
Sandy Schultz, North	71362
Marta Magalhaes, Interamerican	73820
Pat Stephenson, Medical	74147
Nora Murrell, Wolfson	73265
Jeanne Wescott, South	72804

Appendix C2

EPS 591: WORKSHOP IN EDUCATION EFFECTIVE TEACHING AND LEARNING IN HIGHER EDUCATION

Course Description

The course provides participants with the knowledge required to understand teacher characteristics and teaching styles, learner characteristics and learning styles, theories of motivation and their application to the classroom, and strategies for making course content relevant to students; to apply appropriate principles in planning and presenting curricula; to tap into institutional learning resources; and to use effective practical learning/study tools in the classroom. Four assumptions underlie this description:

1. The instructional model for this course emphasizes the practical and the concrete *first* and then provides the necessary theoretical underpinnings, which are drawn from both traditional and nontraditional approaches.

2. The course is divided into seven modules, each of which can be taught independently. The multi-transcultural variations in teaching/learning styles and metacognitive skills are integrated in every module, as are critical thinking skills demonstrated by intellectual curiosity, skepticism, honesty, and respect for other viewpoints.

3. Module assignments require course participants to examine and use their individual classrooms, students, and disciplines as a basis for learning and applying course content.

4. The new teacher taking this course will use this knowledge to become more versatile and be able to assess students for what teaching style will work best; however, in no way will this impinge on academic freedom.

Objectives

Upon completing this course, the participant will have covered seven modules (see outline) designed to help him/her:

1. *Understand Teacher Characteristics and Teaching Styles*
   The course begins with self-exploration of each participant. By means of one or more inventories, participants are able to identify the primary components and biases of their personal teaching style, focus on characteristics they wish to expand or change, and gain a perspective on how their individual style meshes with the overall matrix of teaching styles and assessment. This matrix includes variations in cultural, affective, perceptual, and interpersonal dimensions.

2. *Understand Learner Characteristics and Learning Styles*
   With the personal awareness facilitated by the previous module, participants concentrate on the matrix of learning styles and assessment of learners in general and the students with whom they interact in particular. This matrix, too, includes variations in cultural, affective, perceptual, and interpersonal dimensions. By the end of this module, participants will have been exposed to the need for contextual flexibility and adaptability—both their own and that of their students, whose self-awareness they can play a significant part in expanding and to various instruments they may use to learn about their students. For example, some students learn best in a nurturing and supportive environment, while the quality of the information is a more important factor for other students.

3. *Motivate Students*
   With some understanding of the dynamics involved in teacher-learner interactions, participants study strategies for motivating students. This process requires active steps to identify (a) the levels and types of study skills and learning needs of each student and (b) students' individual and collective values. Given this information, as well as some general theories about motivation, the teacher can adopt measures to help the students learn.

4. *Discover Relevance*

   Once the student's study/learning mode is understood, participants can discover ways to help the student incorporate his/her background and environmental/community context into a personalized learning experience. In this module participants learn how to elicit the information that teachers need and then how to select and use current materials to foster relevancy as a motivational tool. Because a teacher is also called upon to be a role model, he or she should therefore demonstrate a concern both for the classroom community and for life that extends beyond the classroom.

5. *Plan Courses*

   Participants here concentrate on strategies for planning courses effectively and efficiently. Building on a base of information about their students and themselves, and simultaneously incorporating certain concepts about course planning in general, teachers can develop innovative and interesting materials. The concepts embody principles for varying the methods of instructional delivery and assessment, sequencing and pacing the instructional events, and creating continuity with the student's prior learning and with other courses in the sequence.

6. *Develop Practical Applications*

   Although all the modules have a practical application, this one integrates the previous modules in a series of applications that emphasize metacognitive, communication, and critical thinking skills across disciplines. Participants modify and perhaps formalize the list of applications they have been developing and implementing for their individual disciplines.

7. *Apply Institutional Resources to Classroom Teaching/ Learning*

   The resources in this module emphasize technology. Among the topics are CAI (computer-assisted instruction), CMI (computer-managed instruction), test banking, interactive video, audiovisual services, learning centers, computer labs, and institutional research.

Appendix C3

SUBJECT: *Authorization to enter into a contractual agreement with the University of Miami for graduate instruction in the improvement of teaching and learning*

RATIONALE: From the start of the Teaching/Learning Project in 1986 it was clear that, if teaching and learning at Miami-Dade Community College were to be improved, the College would need to provide its faculty with professional development opportunities to help them reach that goal. As the Project progressed and Subcommittees did extensive research, specific recommendations began to emerge: graduate-level courses should be developed to deliver a curriculum designed for the needs of Miami-Dade faculty and Miami-Dade students; all faculty should be encouraged to take these courses, with the College bearing the tuition expense. Included among the proposed faculty advancement policy guidelines that were brought to a referendum of the faculty in April 1989 were ones that called for making completion of two graduate courses on teaching and learning a requirement for new faculty seeking tenure. These policy guidelines were overwhelmingly approved by the faculty.

In 1987 faculty from Miami-Dade and the University of Miami joined together to design the two graduate courses in teaching and learning called for by the Teaching/Learning Project. Both have been completed and were piloted during the 1988 academic year. The College has negotiated with the University of Miami to offer these courses at times and locations (Miami-Dade campuses) that would be convenient for our faculty. Cost, of course, is one of the factors that must be considered. University of Miami tuition for a 3-credit graduate course is $1,300; working professionals pay one-half, or $650. If the College were to pick up the tuition costs of the over-one-hundred new faculty currently on board who are expected to take both courses, the expense clearly would be prohibitive. The University of Miami has agreed, however, to teach these two courses on a contractual basis. The current needs of our faculty can be met if a total of eight sections (three of EPS 595 Classroom Research in the fall and three of EPS 596 Effective Teaching and Learning in the winter; one of each in spring/summer) are scheduled during the 1989 academic year. Irrespective of the number of faculty/students enrolled, the University of Miami would charge the College $7,500 per section.

RECOMMENDATION: The College is authorized to enter into a contractual agreement with the University of Miami for instruction for eight sections of two graduate courses, EPS 595 Classroom Research and EPS 596 Effective Teaching and Learning during the 1989 academic year. The contract year will begin on September 11, 1989. The total cost of the contract will not exceed $60,000.

Appendix C4

MEMORANDUM

DATE: March 22, 1990
TO: M-DCC Faculty and Professional Staff
FROM: Mardee Jenrette
SUBJECT: *Graduate Courses in Teaching and Learning*

Both graduate courses developed cooperatively by M-DCC and the University of Miami through the Teaching/Learning Project will be offered this coming term. The schedule is shown below. These courses are paid for by the College as part of its commitment to professional development. Faculty hired after January 1988 must take these courses to be eligible for continuing contract. They must be given priority for enrollment, but I would encourage everyone to consider taking advantage of this opportunity.

To pre-register, please call Evelyn Avalo at extension 7-3470. You may take both courses during the same term if you wish. If you have any question on this program, please call me at extension 7-3775.

May 16–June 22, 1990 (University of Miami Summer Term)

    EPS 595: Research in the Classroom
    Wolfson Campus, Room TBA
    Mondays and Wednesdays, 1:30 p.m. – 4:00 p.m.

    EPS 595: Effective Teaching and Learning
    Wolfson Campus, Room TBA
    Tuesdays and Thursdays, 1:30 p.m. – 4:00 p.m.

Appendix C5

MIAMI-DADE COMMUNITY COLLEGE
OFFICE OF THE PRESIDENT

MEMORANDUM

DATE: December 13, 1989

TO: Participants in EPS 596: Effective Teaching and Learning

FROM: Mardoo Jonrotto

SUBJECT: *Follow-Up Survey*

Please take a few moments to answer the questions that follow based on your experience as a student in EPS 596. The purpose of conducting this survey is to get the kind of information that will help this course be as relevant to and useful for our faculty as possible. Because that aim is so important to all of us, I hope you will find the time to respond. I am not asking that you sign your form. I hope that you will be detailed and open with your feedback.

Thank you.

SURVEY

The following questions refer to EPS 596: Effective Teaching and Learning in the Community College. (A copy of the course outline is attached to aid your recall.)

1. Were the topics covered in the course relevant to your teaching situation? (Circle appropriate number. Use 1 for most relevant, 5 for irrelevant.)

Unit One	1	2	3	4	5
Unit Two	1	2	3	4	5
Unit Three	1	2	3	4	5
Unit Four	1	2	3	4	5

Unit Five	1	2	3	4	5
Unit Six	1	2	3	4	5
Unit Seven	1	2	3	4	5

Comments: _____

_____

_____

_____

2. Did the assignments and materials presented fulfill your expectations for the topic? (Circle 1 for excellent match, 5 for total mismatch.)

Unit One	1	2	3	4	5
Unit Two	1	2	3	4	5
Unit Three	1	2	3	4	5
Unit Four	1	2	3	4	5
Unit Five	1	2	3	4	5
Unit Six	1	2	3	4	5
Unit Seven	1	2	3	4	5

Comments: _____

_____

_____

_____

INDEX

Administrator Advancement
  Subcommittee, 13
*Administrator excellence,
  Statement of,* 13
Assessing the Portfolio, 104, 106
Centers for Teaching and
  Learning, 10, 11, 12, 64, 83,
  86, 101–102, 103, 104, 108,
  109, 112, 118
College Executive Committee,
  83, 85, 86, 90, 102
college president, 2, 3, 5, 6, 12,
  13, 15, 16, 17, 19, 27, 28, 40,
  45, 61, 62, 63, 64, 65, 66, 67,
  68, 78, 79, 80, 81, 85, 87, 88,
  93, 104, 107, 115, 116
College President's Council, 44,
  45, 48, 61, 69, 84
consultants, 3, 16, 27, 33–34, 37,
  44, 55, 65, 81
continuing contracts, 84, 85, 102,
  104
"Conversation on Teaching and
  Learning," 5, 28, 32, 62, 63
department chairperson, role of,
  13, 113
Department Chairperson
  Compensation/Support
  Committee, 13
District Board of Trustees, 45,
  64, 80, 101
endowed chairs, 9, 10, 12, 20, 40,
  46, 62, 63, 64, 65, 78, 79, 80,
  84, 85, 102, 104, 106, 109, 111

Endowed Chair Committee, 12,
  64, 85, 104
faculty advancement, 9, 11, 12,
  13, 20, 63, 68, 77, 82, 87, 92,
  93, 98, 99, 102, 103, 104, 105,
  106, 107, 108, 109, 110
  philosophical principles, 10
faculty advancement policy, 11,
  12, 108, 110, 111, 120
faculty advancement procedure,
  11, 12, 13, 68, 70, 90, 108,
  110, 111, 112, 120
Faculty Advancement
  Procedures Committee, 62,
  84, 86, 89, 91
*Faculty Advancement Promotions
  Process,* 106
Faculty Advancement
  Subcommittee, 63, 77, 78, 80,
  84, 86, 89, 91
faculty behavior, 41
Faculty Behaviors
  Subcommittee, 42
faculty excellence, 6, 7, 63
Faculty Excellence, Statement of, 7,
  8, 9, 10, 12, 44, 45, 47, 48, 49,
  66, 68, 80, 120
Faculty Excellence Subcommittee, 7, 42, 43, 44, 47, 66, 77,
  78, 83–84, 86, 89, 117
faculty senates, 45, 85, 86, 90, 91,
  102, 104, 105, 106, 113
Faculty Senates' Consortium, 17,
  80, 82, 83, 84, 107

feedback, 12, 19, 107, 109, 111, 116
graduate-level courses, 11, 65
  Assessing Learning in the Community College, 11
  Effective Teaching and Learning in the Community College, 11
Information in Brief, 65
Insight, 65
League for Innovation in the Community College, 17
mentoring program, 9, 62
Miami-Dade Community College Foundation, 12
Monitoring and Review Committee, 12, 70, 84, 85, 86, 98, 105, 108–109
National Training Laboratories, 79
new faculty, 41, 118
New Faculty Orientation Program, 9
New Faculty Subcommittee, 8
non classroom faculty, 13, 29–30
Non Classroom Faculty Subcommittee, 49
Organizing M-DCC to Emphasize Faculty/Student Performance, 15, 28
performance portfolios, 12, 62, 84, 102, 103, 104, 106, 107, 109, 111, 113, 118
performance review, 62, 63, 78, 80, 81, 85, 89, 90, 102, 106
Policy I-80, 40, 41, 42
Project Director, 5, 16, 17, 18, 19, 28, 39, 40, 45, 46, 48, 49, 50, 51, 57, 58, 63, 64, 68, 83, 102, 104, 107, 115, 116, 122
project evolution, 1
project goals, 1, 4, 16, 17, 18, 30, 116, 117, 119, 120, 122

project origins, 1, 3, 12, 18, 20
promotions, 9, 10, 16, 29, 40, 46, 62, 63, 64, 78, 79, 80, 84, 85, 96, 97, 102, 103, 104, 105, 106, 109, 110, 111
  First Year Implementation Report, 106
Steering Committee, 5, 6, 18, 19, 27, 29, 30, 39, 40, 41, 42, 44, 46, 48, 49, 64–65, 70, 77, 82, 83, 84, 103, 106, 109, 116, 118, 119, 120
subcommittee chairs, 41
Support for Faculty Subcommittee, 10
Support Staff Advancement Subcommittee, 13
Support Staff Excellence, Statement of, 13
Taking Teaching Seriously, 62
Teaching and Learning environment, 6, 7, 41
Teaching/Learning Environment Subcommittee, 8
Teaching/Learning Project Bulletin, 29, 44, 62–63, 65, 66, 67, 68–69, 82, 103
Teaching/Learning Project Summary Report, 65
Teaching and Learning relationship, 32
Teaching and Learning values, 9, 10, 29, 41,
  seven institutional values, 6, 120
Teaching and Learning Values Subcommittee, 6, 64
tenure, 9, 10, 16, 28, 40, 46, 62, 63, 64, 78, 79, 80, 85, 105, 106, 109, 110, 111